DATE DUE

APR 0 6 2003			

#47-0108 Peel Off Pressure Sensitive

Mothers and Children Facing Divorce

Research in Clinical Psychology, No. 15

Peter E. Nathan, Series Editor

Professor and Chairman
Department of Clinical Psychology
Rutgers, the State University of New Jersey

Other Titles in This Series

Mothers and Children Facing Divorce.

by
Tracy Barr Grossman

UMI RESEARCH PRESS
Ann Arbor, Michigan

Produced and distributed by
UMI Research Press
an imprint of
University Microfilms, Inc.
Ann Arbor, Michigan 48106

Library of Congress Cataloging in Publication Data

Grossman, Tracy Barr, 1952-.
Mothers and children facing divorce.

(Research in clinical psychology ; no. 15)
Revision of thesis (Ph.D.)—University of Michigan,
1984.
Bibliography: p.
Includes index.
1. Divorced mothers—United States. 2. Children of
divorced parents—United States. 3. Divorce—United
States. 4. Separation (Psychology) I. Title.
II. Series.
HQ834.G765   1986   362.8'2   86-11336
ISBN 0-8357-1767-4 (alk. paper)

Contents

Figures

Tables

Acknowledgments

Work on this book has spanned several years and required the help of numerous people. I would like to thank Martha Ourieff Diamond for her invaluable assistance in interviewing the families, Albert Cain, Neil Kalter, Margery Adelson, and Ann Hartman for their expert guidance at each stage of this research project. This book would not have been possible without the mothers and children who agreed to be interviewed and who willingly reviewed an extremely difficult period of their life so that they might help others in similar circumstances.

1

Introduction

Divorce is a family crisis requiring an extended recovery period. This book focuses on individuals five to eighteen months after the final decree was granted, a time recognized as a transitional phase between the acute upset which accompanies the turmoil of the divorce process and successful adaptation to postdivorce life (Weiss, 1975; Wallerstein and Kelly, 1980). Many of the feelings are still experienced but no longer in an overwhelming manner. The day-to-day demands of living in a single-parent household, however, have fostered an additional set of reactions. The current research is concerned both with mothers' and children's memories of their responses to the separation and the divorce as they were occurring and the range of their feelings about their present situation.

The pervasiveness of divorce in our society makes research in this area imperative. The rate of divorce has risen steadily over the last twenty years; only in the last few years has it begun to level off. Over one million children in the United States are affected annually. Given the large number of people involved and the potential of divorce for the development of psychological problems (Wallerstein and Kelly, 1980), it is important that norms be established for the reactions to different aspects of the divorce process. Only by knowing the different stresses created for parents and children by a divorce can professionals be prepared to help a family deal with them. Likewise, a knowledge of the "typical" responses and their usual duration is necessary for a correct assessment of a family's functioning. Without this knowledge, it is impossible to separate those symptoms which are clearly divorce-related from those which suggest problems of a different nature, and those symptoms which, although severe, are likely to be transitory from those which truly signal chronic difficulties.

By obtaining data from a nonclinical sample, this book aims to describe the reactions to the divorce process experienced by latency-age and preadolescent children and their mothers, and to note the frequency of these reactions. In so doing, it attempts in part to affirm the work of Wallerstein and Kelly (1976, 1980; Kelly and Wallerstein, 1976) on this age group.

Parents and children do not respond to the divorce as isolated individuals. Each person's reactions are influenced by how other family members are coping with this crisis. Moreover, the manner in which a child expresses his distress is determined in large part by the family "rules" for dealing with intense feelings. The rest of the family's reactions also become part of the individual's divorce experience. Family members respond to their perceptions (both accurate and inaccurate) of how the others are feeling in addition to the events themselves. This process continues in an increasingly complex fashion as each person responds to the other's reactions.

This book was designed to study the interrelationship of individual family members' reactions. Mothers' and children's views of each other's reactions are examined as well as their sense of their own experience. Of particular interest are those areas where misperceptions of one's mother's or children's feelings most often occur. It is believed that these misperceptions, as well as accurately perceived differences in reactions between generations, lead to stress (both individual and between family members). Mothers and children are thereby limited in their ability to help one another adapt to the changes they are experiencing. The influence of the sex of the children, sibling position, and the frequency of father-child contact, will be considered as the interaction of individuals' responses is analyzed. It is predicted, in accordance with the findings of earlier studies (McDermott, 1968; Hetherington, 1977, 1978; Wallerstein and Kelly, 1980) that sex will be an important determinant while the effect of sibling position will be negligible. The mother-son relationship will likely be the most stressed. With respect to the different father-child relationships, it is hypothesized that families in which there is consistent and frequent positive contact between father and child will in general function more smoothly—that is, mothers and children will be more attuned to each other—than families in which visitation is sporadic. However, it is also expected that each of the varied postdivorce visitation arrangements will create certain types of stress.

Early Research and Its Limitations

An early focus of research in this field was to compare children from divorced families with children from intact homes to determine whether divorce was detrimental to child development. Most often, this research was conducted with the bias that divorce was either not generally harmful to children (Goode, 1956; 1964) or a preferable alternative to maintaining a home which was "psychologically broken" (Nye, 1957; Landis, 1962). The results typically confirmed the authors' initial beliefs.

While supporting the underlying assertion of Landis and Nye that the degree of predivorce marital strife is a factor in the disturbed development of some children from divorced homes, recent work has generally shown their conclusions to be overgeneralized and misleading. First, although some children adapt successfully to the divorce, many more than is suggested by these early studies are problematically affected by it and exhibit long-standing impaired functioning. This assertion is supported by studies of children who were believed by the researchers involved to represent a nonclinical population and by research which specifically examined a psychiatric population. With regard to the first group of studies, Wallerstein (1977) found that after eighteen months of parental separation, 37 percent of the 131 children studied were assessed to have moderately to severely impaired or significantly uneven ego-functioning. Thirty-two percent of this group had deteriorated one to three steps on a scale of ego functioning since the divorce. This percentage was as large as that of the group that had improved.

In a study of 400 consecutive cases referred to Youth Services of the Department of Psychiatry at the University of Michigan, Kalter (1977) observed that children whose parents had divorced were represented in a psychiatric population at almost two times the rate of the occurrence of divorce in the population at large. Furthermore, these children presented a different pattern of referring problems than children whose parents lived together (presumably many of whom had "unhappy" homes). As a group they displayed more acting-out or predelinquent behavior including running away from home, poor behavior in school (McDermott, 1970) and overt aggression towards parents or peers. Additionally, McDermott found more depression in the divorced group. It was coded as a central problem in 34.3 percent of the divorce cases and found to be present in a hidden or mild form when the records of the entire divorce group were examined. He interpreted the acting-out behavior as most often a defense against hidden depression and a sense of helplessness.

Second, regardless of whether children eventually adapt to parental divorce or benefit by it in the long run, almost all initially experience it as a crisis and react quite severely. Large numbers still show signs of disturbance related to the divorce two years later (Wallerstein and Kelly, 1974, 1975, 1976, 1980; Kelly and Wallerstein, 1976; Hetherington, 1978a, 1978b; McDermott, 1968). Adjustment is difficult and painful even when predivorce family tension had been extreme. Kelly and Wallerstein report in their study on early latency children (1976) "that *none* of the children was pleased or relieved with the divorce, despite a history of many of these families of chronic, often violent marital conflict to which most of the children were witness" (p. 26). Moreover, children commonly consider their predivorce homes to have been happy and/or secure (Landis, 1960; Anthony, 1975; Toomin, 1974) and have not anticipated the divorce.

The Reaction of Children to the Divorce Process

The major portion of the psychological literature on divorce is devoted to listing and describing children's reactions. The separation of the parents and the consequent physical departure of the father (or, in rare instances, the mother) from the household is seen as the central event for children. It is this step of the divorce process which children find most painful. Their psychological responses are commonly noted to approximate a mourning process (Kelly and Wallerstein, 1976; Wallerstein and Kelly, 1976, 1975; Weiss, 1975; Toomin, 1974; Robinson et al., 1973; Sugar, 1970a; Gardner, 1956), paralleling in many ways the reactions of children to the death of a parent. As in the case with a death of a parent, the news of the impending divorce initially elicits disbelief, shock and denial. These early reactions can then be followed by an extensive set of responses including: pervasive depression, longing for the absent parent, idealization of the absent parent, related blaming of custodial parent for divorce and consequent hostile feelings toward her (him), generally heightened anxiety, a sense of helplessness, feelings of rejection, anger stemming from perceived abandonment or frustration of needs, fear of being abandoned (i.e., divorced) by the remaining parent, unrealistic wishes for parental reconciliation, lowered self-esteem, self-blame and related guilt, loss of interest in daily events, somatic symptoms such as loss of appetite, headaches and stomach aches, regression, and defenses against the loss such as undoing the departure in fantasy (Roberts and Roberts, 1974; Weiss, 1975; Anthony, 1974; Sugar, 1970a, Sugar 1970b; Robinson et al., 1973; Bernstein and Robey, 1962; Toomin, 1974; Gardner, 1956; Mohr, 1947; Westman, 1970, 1972).

The analogy of bereavement is not totally apt however, for in divorce the absent parent remains alive and is capable of seeing his children whether or not he chooses to do so. The child must adjust to seeing his father less frequently and alter their relationship accordingly but not emotionally withdraw from him completely (Anthony, 1974). In addition to detailing some of the ways in which the father-child relationship must change, Toomin (1974) spells out the other losses which are inherent in a divorce. Unlike a child's relationship with the "predivorce father," contact with a noncustodial parent is usually more rigid and relegated to carefully restricted time periods. The child therefore needs to wait until he can tell his father about daily activities and then "be close on demand." Roles such as disciplinarian, rescuer in mother-child conflicts, and masculine protector and lender of strength, which may have been played by the father when he was a member of the household are difficult to continue as a visiting parent. Moreover, these roles often can be undermined by the mother's efforts to degrade her ex-husband. Toomin notes that the child's image of the father commonly shifts so that he is either idealized as a means of denying the loss or resentfully rejected.

Another loss for the child is his previously maintained trust that the parental unit would always remain the same and be available to him. Also lost is the child-mother-father relationship. Toomin postulates that parents interacting together impact differently on a child in terms of such developmental issues as the formation of identification patterns, than each alone, particularly when they are disparaging of each other. In day-to-day responsibilities of parenting, the mother and father in a two-parent family both complement and supplement each other in providing support, control, and nurturance. Additionally, the child must "mourn" the loss of the predivorce mother. Because she is adjusting psychologically and practically to her new situation she may be away from the child more often and act differently when she is with him. Finally, the child may lose environmental supports if a move becomes necessary or support figures become unavailable.

Although the act of separation may trigger the most acute response, divorce is not a singular event. It is usually preceded by a long period of hostility or tension between the parents which for some is considered to be equally or more significant to the child's overall adjustment than the divorce itself (Despert, 1953; Anthony, 1974).

The divorce process continues after the separation as well. Neither the embittered nor the loving aspects of the spousal relationship cease abruptly with the termination of the marriage (Goode, 1956). The child must thus continue to cope with emotional and hostile parental interactions for an indefinite period. The presence of children in fact, seems to fuel the parents' postdivorce battles. In examining 148 consecutive divorce cases processed in the Dane County, Wisconsin Family Court, Westman (1970) observed that whereas only 5 percent of the childless couples were involved in litigation after the final decree was granted, 52 percent of the cases with children returned to court. Moreover, 31 percent of this latter group "showed evidence of repeated and intensive interaction between the divorced couple during a two-year period following the divorce decree" (p. 417). Given that no attempt was made to control for length of marriage, it is unknown if this factor also affected whether postdivorce legal contests took place. It is logical that couples married for a longer period would be more likely to have children and also more likely to have difficulties disentangling themselves from a problematic relationship.

A weakness in most of the literature examined up to this point, especially the cluster of studies cited at the end of the list of reactions, is the tendency of authors to treat the children of divorce as a basically uniform group. While the circumstances of the divorce are recognized to differ somewhat (e.g., in terms of the degree and nature of parental hostility), the characteristics of the individual children are not typically taken into account. The relative prominence or even existence of particular reactions is often acknowledged to be dependent on the age of the child, but this variable is only considered in a few instances when the children's divorce experience is actually elucidated. Gardner (1956) describes some of the reactions of "younger" and "older" children. Westman (1972) notes some of the reactions expected at each developmental stage. Other influential factors such as the quality of the early environment, predivorce personality functioning, and the availability of support figures, are also mentioned at the beginning of a few of these studies (Weiss, 1975; Anthony, 1974; Sugar, 1970a; Robinson et al., 1973) but their actual impact on the child's reaction is not discussed.

An additional limitation of these studies is that the data were collected unsystematically and appear to be based in most cases on clinical populations. Typically, the specific source of the author's observations is not even noted and no effort is made to avoid generalizing their findings to all children who experience divorce.

Only three studies have been conducted which attempted to explore systematically the reactions of children from a normal population at the time of parental separation and divorce. McDermott (1968) and Hetherington et al. (1977, 1978a, 1978b), whose work will be referred to in more detail later, succeeded in this goal by basing their studies of the impact of divorce on youngsters attending a normal nursery school. There is some doubt however, as to whether Wallerstein and Kelly's research with children aged two and one-half to eighteen (1974, 1975, 1976; Kelly and Wallerstein, 1976) focused on a truly "normal" population. They did purposefully exclude children with a history of psychological problems in the hope of isolating the effect of the divorce process. Yet, while they profess that this left them with a normal sample, the validity of their assertion is not certain. Although severe problem cases were weeded out, the subjects were obtained through referrals to a "Divorce Counseling Service." This raises the question of whether the families interviewed by Wallerstein and Kelly were unusual in their need and/or desire for counseling. Despite the limitations which this sampling technique places on an interpretation of their findings however, Wallerstein and Kelly's work presents a rich and detailed view of children's feelings, preoccupations, and behavior following divorce. All three of the above-mentioned studies take age into account as a potent factor influencing a child's reactions but only Wallerstein and Kelly examine the importance of a child's developmental stage at several phases of childhood.

Given that this book studies the reactions of latency and preadolescent children, just Wallerstein and Kelly's observations of children aged six to twelve years will be reported now. Based on interviews conducted shortly following the separation, it was concluded that in general, all of these children regard the father's departure from the home (mothers gain custody of their children in over 90 percent of divorce cases) as a personal rejection. They respond at first with disbelief, shock, and denial. All show signs of sadness, loneliness, and fear concerning the uncertain future. The younger children in this sample (i.e., those aged six to eight), however, have considerably greater difficulty obtaining relief from those feelings and are more immobilized by them. Signs of pervasive depression are much more frequent and they are more vulnerable to regression. In contrast, the older latency and preadolescent children are often able soon to perceive clearly and accept the reality. Rather than disorganization, defenses against these feelings are most evident.

Children in the younger group also miss the father acutely, finding visits unsatisfactory, unless they occur several times weekly with both parents' approval. They are also highly defended against expressing anger toward the father. Anger at the mother is sometimes apparent, most often expressed in displacements. More commonly, the children reveal fear of antagonizing the mother and thereby jeopardizing their own security. They are unable to avoid being used by the parents or to reject one parent totally and align with the other. Often, their loyalty conflict is evident even when neither parent seems invested in pushing the child towards such a decision. Fantasies of parental reconciliation are frequent.

The older group feels much more humiliated by the divorce itself, its implied rejection of them, their inability to alter the course of events, and for having revealed their distress. Also unlike the younger children, their anger is conscious, intense, and object-directed. These children typically perceive a choice between excluding or actively rejecting one parent and aligning with the other, or feeling isolated and lonely. Wallerstein and Kelly note that about a quarter of them opt for the first choice soon after the parental separation; many more do so a year later. These alignments tend to consolidate over time. A final characteristic reaction of children aged nine to twelve years is the development of pseudoadolescent and adult behavior. These children often become emotional supports for their parents as well as a source of advice and practical help.

These findings of Wallerstein and Kelly were derived from the first phase of a five-year longitudinal study. The second set of interviews took place approximately one year after the initial research or about a year and one-half after the separation. Most of the divorces had become final prior to this follow-up. The time of Wallerstein and Kelly's follow-up interviews, in relation to the granting of the divorce papers, corresponds closely to the time in which the interviews for this study took place.

Wallerstein and Kelly (1980) found that by the time of the second set of interviews, a majority of their total child sample had progressed beyond the acute phase of reacting to the divorce process. Crisis-evoked responses such as fear, grief, and shock had lessened or disappeared altogether. In general, feelings about the divorce had changed considerably. Most of the children were no longer unhappy; the percentage of unhappy children in the sample had been reduced by half since the initial contact (from one-half to one-fourth of the sample). However, this improvement in mood did not mean that the children were no longer reacting to the divorce.

> The diminution of crisis-related behavior and symptoms and the greater modulation of emotional responses failed perhaps to catch the still very sober, even sometimes somber feelings these children projected (p. 169).

The major psychopathological finding at the time of the follow-up was childhood depression, present in one-fourth of the children. Latency-age and preadolescent children were disproportionately represented in this depressed group. Of the moderately depressed boys and girls, a large number had been between seven and ten years of age when the separation took place. When the ages of the severely depressed children were determined, it became evident that most of these troubled youngsters were preadolescent boys. The divorce was still the primary preoccupation of these children and sorrow over the departure of the father had not diminished. In general, depression was linked with intense anger, a strong sense of rejection by one or both parents, and a continuing disapproval of the divorce. Since depression was not a common reaction of this age group when the separation first took place, the increase in depression apparent eighteen months later is surprising. It seems to indicate that either the successful defenses described by Wallerstein and Kelly at the time of the first interview had disintegrated as the divorce dragged out so that an underlying depression was exposed or that this depression occurred in response to postdivorce stresses.

In looking at the course of angry feelings about the divorce, the pattern of change over time was similar. Overall, both the number of children who felt angry and the severity of their anger had decreased. Yet, anger had not diminished to the extent that Wallerstein and Kelly had expected. One-fourth of the sample, as compared with one-third at the initial assessment, remained intensely angry. Again, this time along with adolescent girls, the children whose anger remained "most visible and most maintained its initial force" (p. 172) were the original nine- to twelve-year-olds. Moreover, some of the children in the nine- to twelve-year-old group appeared more angry at the follow-up than they had shortly after the separation. Frequent explosive outbursts at their parents were common for preadolescent boys.

In contrast to the significant change in feelings for the majority of the child sample, their attitude about the divorce altered little. Two-thirds of the children still expressed the belief that their current situation was no improvement over the predivorce family. They pragmatically accepted the decision of the divorce but continued to feel it was a bad one. Attitudes towards their parents did change somewhat. Respect for their mother and trust in her had increased although a concomitant shift in feeling did not occur with regard to their father. In fact, the father became "less acceptable as a role model" (p. 174).

Previous Findings on Children's Reactions

The Impact of Sex Differences

The findings regarding sex differences, both in individual responses and in family interactions, are quite consistent. In the immediate aftermath of the divorce, boys appear to have more acute reactions and to become involved in more problematic relationships with their mothers. This issue has been addressed by McDermott (1968), Hetherington (1977, 1978) and Wallerstein and Kelly (1974, 1975, 1976, 1980, Kelly and Wallerstein, 1976).

In his study of 16 preschoolers attending a private nursery school for normal children at the time their parents separated and divorced, McDermott concluded that to a large extent boys and girls respond to divorce with different patterns of behavior. Based on an examination of ongoing anecdotal records kept by teachers over a period of ten years, he observed that boys exhibited more "dramatic changes in behavior, characterized by the abrupt release of aggressive and destructive feelings" (p. 125). They more commonly showed indications of depression such as suddenly breaking into tears for no apparent reason or losing the capacity to play creatively. Girls more typically became sulky, petulant, bossy and pseudomature. McDermott hypothesized that although the boys' reactions appeared more severe at the time of the divorce, the girls' reactions suggest a potentially more serious disturbance.

Similarly, Hetherington, in a multimethod study of 48 sets of divorced parents and their preschool children, observed that most of the negative child behaviors coded were more commonly manifested in boys. In terms of a pattern of specific behaviors, boys from divorced homes were more oppositional and aggressive, while girls were more whining and compliant. While stress in parent-child relations was evident in the divorce process as a whole, particularly at one year postdivorce, this stress was most extreme between mothers and sons. An analysis of the mothers' diary records revealed that mothers of sons felt more anxious, depressed, angry, rejected and incompetent. These negative feelings were especially prevalent when they wrote about interactions with their sons. Furthermore, indications of "poor parenting" such as inconsistency in discipline, and lack of affection were more extreme with sons.

At first glance, the findings of Wallerstein and Kelly appear somewhat different but moving in the same direction. They found few sex differences shortly following the parental separation but significant ones eighteen months later. However, although their findings might not have been replicated had McDermott and Hetherington observed their subjects at an earlier date, the available data suggest that the findings of the three studies are in fact very similar. In other words, Wallerstein and Kelly discovered that sex differences, while not apparent at the beginning of the divorce process, had crystalized by the time the divorce was legalized or soon thereafter, the point at which McDermott and Hetherington conducted their research. These comparisons must be regarded cautiously since the methods and samples of the three projects varied considerably. For example, Wallerstein and Kelly based their findings on open-ended interviews with children aged two and one-half to eighteen years while Hetherington utilized several more objective measures with just preschool children. Yet, it seems noteworthy that three groups of researchers with such vastly different data bases should arrive at similar conclusions.

According to Wallerstein and Kelly (1980), boys seemed to have far more difficulty than girls in adjusting to the divorce. In an analysis of the follow-up interviews, boys were significantly more opposed to the divorce than their sisters, "more stressed," and more preoccupied with the divorce. Boys more frequently longed intensely for their father, felt rejected by their father, continued to fantasize about a parental reunion, and exhibited depressive behavior. Girls on the other hand, were happier and also more likely to view the divorce as an improvement over their family situation prior to the separation. Girls had more friends and demonstrated an ability to use their friends as a support system. In general, girls appeared to be coping more successfully.

Wallerstein and Kelly attempted to discern the reason for the poorer functioning of boys but remained puzzled. They hypothesized that girls may simply be "more resilient that boys in their psychological functioning" (p. 166). Alternatively, they wondered if a more supportive relationship with their parents was responsible for the greater improvement in functioning observed in girls, but evidence was inconsistent. The interviews with parents suggested that girls were treated more benignly and protected more frequently from family battles. However, most of the differences in mothering witnessed by the researchers were clearly attributed to age, not sex (i.e., the mothers were more sympathetic towards the younger children). The boys and girls did not report differences in the manner in which their parents behaved towards them.

Sibling Position

Only Wallerstein and Kelly make reference to the effect of sibling position. They state that sibling position did not seem to impact on the nature of the child's reaction. Since they did not discuss changes in family relationships other than whether a child and parent became closer or more distant, it is not clear if sibling position is an influential factor.

Father-Child Contact

With respect to father-child contact, they report that children find it exceedingly difficult to adjust to the changed relationship with their father regardless of the visitation arrangements. For preschool children, even an improved father-child relationship (i.e., cases where fathers become more affectionate and more consistent in their parenting) does little to prevent serious deterioration in the child's functioning. "An improved emotional interchange between father and child during visits cannot bridge for the preschool child, the separations of time and physical unavailability which the postdivorce structure imposes" (1975, p. 613). Visiting regularly with the father also is little comfort to latency-age children. As mentioned earlier, the only children who found their relationship to their father to be gratifying were those who could see him spontaneously and on their own, several times a week and for whom such frequent visits had the approval of both parents. Visits in fact, often provoke a great deal of stress, as they are times when the parents' continuing bitter and hostile feelings toward each other are expressed.

One aspect of a larger study (Jacobson, 1978a) attempted to determine the relationship between a child's psychosocial adjustment (as measured through the use of parental report via the Louisville Behavior Checklist) and the extent of the decrease in the amount of time spent in the company of and sharing an activity with each parent. Her research focused on 30 families with a total of 51 children, aged three to seventeen years, who had experienced a parental separation within the last year. Half of these families were involved in crisis-oriented treatment while the others were drawn from the divorce population at large. The degree of time lost with the father is clearly an indication of the frequency of visitation.

Examination of the data showed that 42 children spent less time per week with their father after the separation than they did while he still lived with them. Thirty-three children spent fewer hours engaged in activity with him but the actual number of hours lost was minimal. It appears that while children see their father for fewer hours, these hours are more likely to be filled with father-child "activity." The results of Pearson Product-Moment Correlations between time and activity lost with the father and the current social adjustment of the child showed that "there is a consistent indication that the more time lost in the presence of father since the marital separation, the higher the maladjustment of the child" (p. 352). Associations were significant in the areas of aggression (-0.39, $p \leq 0.01$), inhibition (-0.38, $p \leq 0.01$), cognitive disability (-0.46, $p \leq 0.01$), and overall security level (-0.39, $p \leq 0.01$). Although time spent with mother was also lost after the separation, no clear-cut associations with child adjustment were seen. The results concerning loss in activity were in a similar direction but less striking.

The findings of Jacobson's study are somewhat contradictory to the conclusions of Wallerstein and Kelly. While not negating Wallerstein and Kelly's contention that adjustment to seeing the father just on visits is difficult, she does indicate that variations in visiting arrangements are more important than Wallerstein and Kelly lead us to believe. In fact, Jacobson's analysis suggests that a major factor in a child's ability to adjust to divorce is the amount of contact between father and child. (No analysis pertaining to the possible impact on these findings of the sex of the child was performed so it is unknown if these overall findings obscure sex differences.) Regular visitation appears crucial if the child is to resume normal functioning.

The Reactions of Adults to the Divorce Process

A complete detailing of an adult's reactions to divorce is provided by Weiss (1975). In his book *Marital Separation,* Weiss describes the prominent reactions of adults at different points in the divorce process. By the time legal proceedings are under way, the divorcing couple has typically already gone through a "long and anguished process of mutual alienation" which hurts both members of a marital pair and sharply lowers self-esteem (p. 28). Although feelings of love are waning, "attachment" continues so the partners still feel dependent on each other. Commonly, in order to protect oneself from further hurt and because of pride, attachment feelings are hidden behind a facade of indifference. Yearning may appear sporadically or anger may erupt which stems from feelings of rejection or resentment for this continued dependence. After the separation, anger often serves to assist the adult in psychologically separating from the ex-spouse. Feelings at this time consist of deep sadness, regret for lost chances of happiness, fear of being alone and of the unknown problems of single life, and feelings of worthlessness. Guilt and remorse are present, most frequently for the spouse who has initiated the divorce. Sometimes, the separation is followed by feelings of euphoria. Typically, the euphoria, like the anger, is in large part a way of managing the loss by denying its importance. It often alternates with the feelings of distress described above. Generally, extraordinary ambivalence toward the spouse continues for a long time. Strong positive feelings continue to exist alongside equally tenacious negative feelings. Weiss notes that companionship may develop again but true friendship is rarely possible because these mixed feelings cannot be completely disregarded. Negative feelings are frequently given expression around issues concerning the children since this is where the relationship needs to continue.

Loneliness follows "separation distress," occurring in response to both "emotional isolation" (a term coined by Weiss to denote the state when a specific object is no longer the focus of a divorcing person's thoughts) and "social isolation." It is intensified by anxiety about being alone which stems from a view that the world is a frightening place. Sexual needs also get intermeshed with feelings of loneliness.

The social isolation experienced by divorced women has been elaborated by Weiss in *Going It Alone,* and by others (Bohannan, 1979; Miller, 1979). Bohannan contends that the individual's need to cope with a "community divorce" compounds his or her difficulty in dealing with the many aspects of divorce which center around the spouse. Relationships with married friends, especially those which previously revolved around only couple activities, become strained. The divorcée feels upset because she feels marginal to the experiences of her married friends. Get-togethers make her feel more alone. Friends, in addition to being uncomfortable about when to include the divorcée, may feel threatened by her. Women become concerned that their husband may be attracted to her. Men are afraid that she will influence their wives to become more independent.

While the single parent has become isolated from her former support network, her need for ties outside her family has increased. Friends must now provide the help and companionship which she lacks without a husband. Weiss states that the woman's "emotional equilibrium" is dependent on her finding one or two individuals whom she can regularly use as confidantes. Because other divorced women share her experiences and her outlook, her new community is likely to consist of others in similar circumstances.

Although Weiss's description of adults' reaction to divorce is derived from a normal population (he utilized individual and group interviews from a variety of sources although relying primarily on members of Parents Without Partners), it is not based on a systematic investigation. The proportion of divorcing parents who experience any particular response or express their feelings in a particular way, is not known.

The Experience of Adults in the Transitional Phase of Reacting to Divorce

The process of recovering from the crisis of a divorce and adapting to life as a single parent is not a smooth one. For a long period of time, a sense that one is truly in control of circumstances alternates with a fear of being overwhelmed with bad feelings. Weiss (1975) comments that from his observation it takes two to four years before adjustment to the divorce is complete (i.e., before an individual "reestablishes a coherent and stable identity" and a "stable life pattern"). Wallerstein and Kelly (1980) elaborated in detail the psychological functioning of parents during this transitional period. In examining the interviews with the parents of the children described earlier, conducted eighteen months after separation, they found that the typical mother in their sample felt happier and more competent as a single parent than she did a year earlier. Yet, some anxiety about living alone and raising children without her husband was still present. Hopeful feelings about the future were evident although not expressed with certainty.

For a substantial number of women, problems clearly remained. Almost one-half of the mothers were depressed to "some considerable degree," 17 percent extremely so. In many cases, this depression had its origins prior to the divorce although it may have lessened since then. Others were depressed for the first time or had actually become more depressed as time elapsed. The women's depression was attributed to feelings of abandonment, the inability to derive satisfaction from life as a single woman in the way expected, and/or being overwhelmed by the daily pressures of divorced life. Loneliness was even more prevalent, being present for two-thirds of the women and severe for one-third of the sample. Although most women had established a social life by the time of the interview, relationships were short-lived and, for the most part, ungratifying. Finally, one-half of the mothers still routinely made "extremely critical or disparaging remarks" about their ex-spouse. One-fifth of the mothers remained intensely angry to the point that they appeared disorganized in their general psychological functioning.

Although the instances are less frequent than those where the individual continues to suffer from the breakup of her marriage, some women had reportedly reached closure on the divorce process. Many of these individuals viewed the divorce in a mainly positive light. A little less than one-fourth of the women interviewed by Wallerstein and Kelly described their divorce as "an experience of personal growth." It had provided them with the impetus to examine their contribution to a problematic relationship and to change so that their life as a whole had improved. A slightly smaller number of women— 20 percent of the sample—exhibited a major positive change in their parenting ability. They insisted that the freedom from a relationship of conflict allowed them to invest themselves more fully in their children. They enjoyed parenting more and believed they did the job better. Although Wallerstein and Kelly did not note the exact degree of overlap between these two groups of women, they did state that the ability to function better as a parent was linked in many cases with an initial view of the divorce as an opportunity to improve one's life. Moreover, no parents who remained extremely angry at each other or who exhibited "significant psychological disturbance" were seen to have derived increased satisfaction from being a parent or to be functioning better in that role.

The relatively high number of women who still experienced difficulty coping with their life as a divorced mother a year and one-half after their separation can be explained in part by the numerous stresses inherent in the life of a divorced parent. First, economic hardship is common. The incomes of single-parent families are notoriously less than two-parent families (Brandwein et al., 1974). Brandwein notes that in 1972 a study showed that women were typically awarded less than 35 percent of their ex-husband's income as child support payments. Plus, in many cases, even this amount is not paid on a regular basis.

The need to work fulltime for economic reasons leads to the second major stress on single parents: overwhelming responsibilities (Glasser and Navarre, 1965; Weiss, 1979). The divorced mother must accomplish the same tasks that were previously shared between two people. While parallels to the life of a married working mother exist, the situations are far from identical. Although the women in both situations work fulltime, find alternative sources of childcare during the day, and return home at night tired but with the house and children needing attention, the divorced woman is totally on her own. However minimally the married woman's husband participates in household duties, he is present to lend a hand if his wife is feeling overwhelmed. He also is likely to take care of the children for part of the evening even if only to play with them, and to attend to the more traditionally male responsibilities of maintaining a house (e.g., taking out the garbage, doing repairs). Finally, he is an emotional support for his wife and a companion who is readily available. Given that it is physically impossible for the single mother to do everything and that the time given to work is structured and uncompromisable, it is likely that the home activities will be neglected to some degree. Women who prided themselves on an immaculate home may have difficulty accepting the impossibility of maintaining their previous standards but the inability to give as much attention to the children as considered important or desirable may cause considerable guilt.

Although dating is not intrinsically a stress, and may in fact do much to alleviate the feeling of stress connected to other aspects of the divorce process, it does also create its own problems (Weiss, 1979). The guilt the mother experiences because of her reduced time and energy for the children is exacerbated by her choice to spend even more time away from them, this time just for her own pleasure. The children's objections to her dating may add to the mother's hesitancy about getting involved with new people.

The Interaction between Children's and Mothers' Responses to Divorce

Until the last few years, the literature on divorce was oriented almost exclusively to the effect on individual family members. A relationship between the parents' and children's reactions was recognized by some authors but rarely elaborated. Most commonly noted was the negative impact on children of the mother's self-absorption as she attempted to deal with her own pain. Stress reduces the mother's capacity to parent in general and to provide support around divorce-related issues, thus increasing the trauma for the child (Bernstein and Robey, 1962; Despert, 1953; Westman, 1970; Toomin, 1974; Wallerstein and Kelly, 1974, 1975, 1976; Kelly and Wallerstein, 1976). The mother's recognition of the child's needs following the separation is the single most significant factor in the child's ability to cope successfully with the divorce. In case studies of children who were parented both attentively and neglectfully prior to the divorce, it is clearly seen that postdivorce events have far more impact on child functioning than the predivorce circumstances.

When the families of the children who exhibited signs of depression or intense anger a year and one-half after the separation were studied, a pattern of continued hostility between the parents and parental preoccupation with the divorce was evident. Parents were not supportive of their children and seemed unable to be sensitive to the children's pain. Children felt rejected by one or both parents. Overall, the children had experienced a "severe decline in parenting."

Even in cases where the parents' reactions are not so extreme or are only intense for a relatively brief period of time, they influence the children's response to the divorce. Wallerstein and Kelly (1980) observed that a mother's perceptions of her children and her manner of dealing with them, directly related to her own reactions. First, the mother's role in initiating the divorce is an important factor in determining whether she sees the children as coping successfully or being unduly stressed. Mothers who wanted to divorce are more likely to believe that the former case is true; mothers who opposed the divorce tend towards the latter view. The child's actual feelings are obscured. Anger towards the ex-spouse is also likely to be reflected in the mother's attitude toward her children. She may view one child as behaving like the father and act negatively towards him as a result. Alternatively, she may become critical of her son simply because he is male or reject the child who is believed to be aligned with the father. In all of the above cases the child is likely to feel that his mother is insensitive to his feelings and possibly withdrawn from him.

Finally, the loneliness and isolation of the parent at the time of the divorce may lead her to perceive the children as capable of providing support and companionship in an adult manner. Children are induced to bolster the mother's self-esteem and to prevent depression from taking hold. Adult issues of an intimate or financial nature are shared with the impression that the children comprehend the mother's dilemmas and can offer solutions. In the short-run, children seem to be capable of truly helping the parent. Wallerstein and Kelly found that children learned to protect their parents from pressure and could aid in "stabilizing parents' moods and anchoring them to the here and now." By parenting their parent, they made the mother's situation manageable for her. The children, in turn, became more mature, empathic individuals and were proud of their important role in the family. However, when they were used inappropriately as confidantes or this role reversal was maintained beyond the crisis period of the divorce, the children were unable to resume healthy developmental progress.

In terms of the children's impact on the adult's reaction, it has already been shown that the simple presence of children in the family creates stresses for the mother. Weiss (1975, 1979) discussed the problems of task overload, interference with forming new heterosexual relationships, and unending responsibility.

On the positive side, children's need for their mother's continuing care is helpful in the mother's attempt to cope with the divorce. It provides a structure to her life which makes functioning easier and underlines that she is important to someone. Additionally, the children give assurance that she is valued and loved (Weiss, 1975). It was the ability of some children to be acutely sensitive to their mother's needs that was the factor, in the mother's view, which made survival following the separation possible.

Although Weiss is cognizant of the impact of having young children on a woman's divorce experience, he does not examine the effect on the mother of the children's reactions to the divorce process. In general, this issue has been given very little attention. Wallerstein and Kelly (1980) commented that mothers sometimes find it extremely difficult to cope with their children's depression. In extreme cases, intolerance leads to physical abuse. Toomin (1974) noted that the child's tendency to idealize his father is stressful for the mother, especially when the child begins to emulate qualities of the father. The child's efforts to hold onto the father are at cross-purposes to the mother's wish to detach herself from him.

Studies Focusing on the Interrelationship of Children's and Mothers' Reactions to Divorce

Studies which deal specifically with the complex interplay of parents' and children's reactions to the divorce process are extremely limited. The one clinically based study which refers to the interrelationship of a mother and child's responses following divorce is provided by Tooley (1976). She became interested in the symptom picture of a group of boys, aged four to seven years, who lived with their mothers and had minimal contact with their fathers. They were referred to Children's Psychiatric Hospital in Ann Arbor, Michigan for being physically aggressive, defiant, bossy and bullying, unmanageable, and hyperactive. After some therapeutic work it became apparent that the child's aggressive, masterful style was actually a facade designed to reassure himself, intimidate others and "keep the weak, helpless frightened self well hidden" from a threatening world. An examination of the mother showed her to be extremely passive and very conflicted about becoming more assertive and aggressive as her new situation warranted. A family pattern thus emerged where the mother inappropriately shifted the responsibility of being assertive to her son. He would then try to accommodate her, while simultaneously acting upon his own anger, but achieved only a child's results. He got into trouble at school and in the neighborhood, provoking counteraggressions. This caused the mother and son to withdraw more dramatically. A mother's encouraging her son to become the "man of the house" is a reaction noted by others as well (Roberts and Roberts, 1974; Westman, 1972; McDermott, 1970) but only Tooley attempts to describe this as being the result of an interaction between two people.

Hetherington (1977, 1978a, 1978b) conducted a research project which had as its primary focus the impact of divorce on family functioning. Her aim was to compare families of divorce to intact families in order to discern differences between the two groups. The impact of the child's sex on family interactions was also a consideration. Over the course of two years, she therefore studied 96 families, all of whom had a child in nursery school: 24 were families who had experienced divorce and had a daughter, 24 were families who had experienced a divorce and had a son, and so on. In all divorced families, the mother had custody of her children. These families were studied through a variety of techniques including observations of child and parent interactions and of the child at school, interviews with the parents, and structured diary records by the parents.

Hetherington found that households of the divorced subjects were always more disorganized. Moreover, interaction patterns between divorced parents and their children were significantly different from those in intact families on almost all variables examined. Differences were less extreme but still evident at the end of the second year postdivorce. Hetherington observed that divorced parents made fewer maturity demands of their children, communicated less well, tended to be less affectionate, displayed marked inconsistency in discipline, and in general demonstrated a lack of control over their children. In the lab situation, divorced mothers tried to control their children by being more restrictive and giving more commands than nondivorced mothers. Divorced mothers also used more negative sanctions although positive sanctions became more frequent after the first year. In turn, children from divorced families ignored or resisted their mother more frequently. They also appeared more dependent, disobedient, aggressive, whining, demanding, and unaffectionate. As stated previously, when sex differences in reactions were discussed, stress in parent-child relations was most intense between mothers and sons.

The data suggest that the negative parenting behavior and the negative child behavior occurred in interaction with each other. At each time period, poor parenting was highly correlated with poor behavior on the part of the child. Hetherington concludes that parents and children, especially mothers and sons, become involved in a coercive cycle which escalates in the first year after the divorce.

As indicated earlier, Hetherington's main interest was in determining differences in family functioning between divorced and intact families. She thus treats the divorced families only as a group and bases her report on what appear to be the "average" responses. Although commenting that "wide variations in coping and parenting" occur in both her normal and divorced sample, she makes no attempt to delineate these. Also, although restricting her child sample to first- or second-born children, she never indicates whether sibling position in any way affected the nature of parent-child relationships.

Dimensions of This Study in Relation to Previous Work in the Field

The aim of the current research is to clarify the experience of children and mothers in the period following a parental separation and divorce. This study combines the various perspectives of Wallerstein and Kelly, Weiss, and Hetherington in its interest in both the individual family members and the interrelationship of their reactions. A family's response to divorce is conceptualized as occurring on several levels, all of which need to be examined if a full picture of the divorce process is to emerge. The various chapters of this book are conceived as building blocks in this effort. After a brief look at some characteristics which differentiate the families studied, data analysis will move gradually from a concern with the individual reactions of mothers and children to an increasingly interactive focus. The last two chapters involve an examination of the way in which the individual reactions discussed initially (and each person's perceptions of them) fit together and impact on family functioning. The book's emphasis is on elaborating what actually occurs in the aftermath of a divorce with the hopes of finally describing a family's experience with realistic complexity.

The portion of this book dealing with the individual reactions of mothers and children is based on interviews with families sampled from the general divorced population of Washtenaw County, Michigan. By examining a representative group of individuals, this research will offer insight into the typical reactions of latency and preadolescent children and their mothers. Wallerstein and Kelly's detailed descriptions of children's responses and Weiss's observations of adults dealing with divorce will then serve as a comparison for the current findings.

The selection of variables explored in this research was based on the expected responses of individuals to the various stresses inherent in the divorce process, many of which have been outlined in previous work (Weiss 1976, Hetherington et al., 1977, 1978a). Stress was seen as occurring with regard to three aspects of functioning: psychological, interpersonal (e.g., loss of prior social support system) and practical (e.g., financial difficulties). The choice of psychological reactions studied was guided by an understanding of the components of a grief and mourning process which parallels the response to the loss of the predivorce husband/father. Subjects were thus queried about such responses as longing for the absent parent, feelings of rejection, lowered self-esteem, anger and guilt. Also taken into account was the unique way that divorce modifies and complicates an individual's loss reaction in that parental separation is a planned ending of the marriage, actively pursued by at least one member of the couple. Reactions such as anger and guilt are thus believed to be central to the divorce experience.

The present research will also examine the interaction of mothers' and children's reactions. Hetherington noted a high correlation between poor parenting and negative child behavior following divorce. It is believed that these negative interactions are in part due to the incompatibility of many of the parent and child individual reactions to the divorce process and the consequent difficulties in understanding, sympathizing with, supporting, and/or accurately perceiving what the other is experiencing. This book will not only look at the nature of behavioral changes in the mother-child relationship but also at how each family member views the others' reactions and reacts to them.

2

The Range of Possibilities

Any discussion of a family's reaction to divorce needs to be prefaced by an acknowledgment of the heterogeneity of the population involved. Despite the tendency of most of the literature in the field to treat divorcing families as a uniform group responding to a uniform situation, the divorce experience presented in this research differed from family to family. An examination of the various factors which account for these differences is important in order to understand the range of individual and family reactions to the divorce. A review of the many elements which distinguish one family from another is also important as context for discussion of those reactions which appear in the large majority of cases following divorce. The repeated occurrence of certain responses in spite of vastly different circumstances speaks to the central significance of the divorce event itself (that is, the separation of the parents and the subsequent basic shift in the child-parent relationship).

This book cannot give an in-depth analysis of all these differences, but will describe which ones truly impact on a family's functioning and likewise, which ones appear to have little effect. As will be the case in subsequent chapters, the focus of discussion will be on the nature of the individual reactions of mothers and children, and their interaction during the divorce process. Conclusions are clearly restricted to what can be gleaned from the interviewee's self-reports. In large part, this chapter is designed to sketch out issues which require further analysis and suggest future research.

Variations in How the Divorce Was Initiated

The factors with the most powerful impact on family functioning postseparation appear to be which parent initiated the divorce proceedings and the circumstances under which this occurred. Four basic possibilities exist: the mother can unilaterally initiate the divorce; the mother can initiate the divorce after being provoked to do so by the father; the father can unilaterally initiate the divorce; or the couple can mutually make the decision. (It needs to be recognized that the actual decision to divorce is one step in a very complex process in which the initiator of the marriage breakdown is difficult to assess.) As reported by the mothers interviewed for this project, women made the decision to divorce almost twice as often as men did (21 women as compared with 13 men).[1] However, in nine of these cases the woman only insisted on divorce because of a specific act of her husband: in seven cases she learned that the husband was having an affair; in two cases the husband became severely physically abusive of her. Divorces seemed to occur less frequently (only six couples in this study) because a husband and wife mutually agreed that this would be the desirable alternative. In fact, in the majority of families where, according to the mother, one of the parents came to the conclusion that he/she wanted a divorce, the other parent objected to the plan and/or was totally unprepared when it was suggested. This was true even when the husband had been involved in an extramarital relationship.

Weiss (1975), the one investigator who attempted to discuss the effect of who made the decision to divorce on the adults' reaction, referred to the predominance of certain reactions. He stated that the "leaver" is more likely to feel guilty, while the "left" is more likely to suffer from feelings of rejection and low self-esteem. This was basically true for the current sample but needs to be clarified. While women who were left typically did find it easier to deny responsibility for the divorce and feel less guilty about its consequences, this group included several depressed or masochistic women who blamed themselves for everything that had happened. In spite of the fact that they had made every effort to please their husbands and stand by them, even in situations where it was difficult to understand why they stayed in their marriage, they spent hours berating themselves for failing their husbands and causing them to seek a divorce. Many women whose husbands unilaterally chose to obtain a divorce, were content with their traditional housewife-mother role and found it very difficult to change their lifestyle by returning to work. These women often experienced tremendous guilt for leaving their children during the day and thus abandoning what they believed to be their primary responsibility. Additionally, in cases where the mother left because she was provoked to do so by the father, she often felt quite guiltless.

In terms of Weiss's reference to feelings of rejection and low self-esteem, while it is true that all women who were left experienced these feelings, most of the remaining women described having these reactions as well. The major difference between the two groups with regard to these specific reactions was one of timing. Whereas those "left" felt rejected and unlovable most acutely following their husband's departure, the "leavers" commonly felt this way during the marriage. Many described years of loneliness and rejection within the marriage (e.g., several couples had ceased having a sexual relationship long before the wife filed for a divorce) which made them doubt their own desirability. In cases where the husband had one or a series of affairs, the woman also responded with feelings of rejection and self-doubt. Typically, these feelings shortly preceded the separation and were a major impetus to obtaining the divorce. Those who made the decision to divorce jointly with their husbands responded similarly to the "leavers" although it needs to be stressed that for all these women the reactions did not disappear at the moment the separation took place.

Differences in timing related to whether or not the individual initiated the divorce are not limited to the reactions just described. With regard to all the feelings which accompany the loosening of attachment process such as sadness, anger, moodiness, fear of the future, sense of isolation, and relief, those women with an active role in the decision making surrounding the divorce appeared to be able to resolve a great deal before the separation took place. They were able to deal with those feelings directly related to the thought of terminating their marriage at a separate point from when they needed to learn to cope with the stresses of being a single parent. The women who were unprepared for their husband's decision to end the marriage reportedly had to deal with all these issues at once. Furthermore, the "leaver," having more control over the situation, seemed better able to pace her emotional withdrawal from her husband. The process of letting go tended to be spread out over a longer period of time than was typical of the case for the "left." Of the 27 women who actively sought the divorce (21 independently, six in conjunction with their husband's efforts), 18 specifically stated that it took years to come to their decision or to go ahead with concrete plans once they had decided. For example, one woman described a fairly common situation as follows:

It was about five years before I filed for a divorce. I knew that I was going to do it. It was just a matter of doing the specific things that I felt I should have done before. . . . When I first noticed that I was really unhappy with my husband was when my little one was just a baby, three or four months old. I thought "well here I am, I've got a baby, what can I do?" So I would think about it and think about it and I thought well, I really felt I owed Bobby as much of myself as I had given to John [older child]. I felt that I should be home with him during a good portion of his formative years. But then I really didn't have any type of way to support myself because I had been to college for three years and was a drama major and then dropped out when I got married. So I didn't have a degree and really wasn't trained to do anything and I thought "Oh I have to do something to be able to support us" so I decided to go to nursing school. So I put in my application and waited a year and a half and went and got my nursing degree and then worked part time until Bobby was in kindergarten and then I filed for a divorce. So there was a lot of things—there were times within those five years when I would say "oh today wasn't so bad, I really shouldn't do this" but most of the time I knew that I was just waiting until Bobby was older and I had a career and then I would file. And that's what I did.[2]

As a result of this extension of the time allowed to adjust to the idea of divorce and the greater control involved, these adults were less likely to feel traumatized. Feelings in general were experienced less intensely. Conversely, the women who were passive recipients of the divorce decision stated that they were often overwhelmed by their pain.

I definitely didn't want it and I felt very, very left out, rejected. . . . for the first year I felt very lonely and like I didn't have anything left, you know, and everything was gone. That there wasn't much sense in trying to start over with the kids and what would be different with anyone else.

Clearly, the degree of preparedness for their husband's "news" ranged considerably and was a factor affecting the women's ability to cope with the separation.

The letting go process described for the "leavers" is somewhat modified in instances where the individual begins to consider a divorce at the point that she learns of her husband's illicit affair. These women experienced a sudden hurt much like those "left" and tended to feel emotionally overwhelmed at that time but they usually allowed themselves a recovery period before actually going ahead with the divorce. The "mourning" aspects of dealing with a divorce (i.e., the gradual withdrawal of active feeling for the spouse) still preceded the separation in large part and some control over the pacing of events was maintained.

You know my ex-husband was seeing another girl at that time and it had been going on for a long time. It was two years before I finally admitted it and filed for the divorce. . . . I mean it was obvious but I just wasn't ready to accept it. . . . I was hurt very bad the first time that I had realized, you know, that something was going on. And the hurt was so bad. . . . And then it reached a point where it just didn't matter, you know, that as far as I was concerned the kids and I were living our life and he was living his and we just all lived in the same house when he was around.

The issues of the timing and intensity of the adult's reactions to the divorce have critical consequences for the parent-child relationship pre- and postdivorce, and the manner in which a family as a whole copes with this crisis. The experience of mothers whose husband initiated the divorce most closely parallels the experience of most of the children. Like their children, these mothers may have been aware of tensions in the marriage but rarely considered that a divorce would be forthcoming. As a result the basic timetable for reactions is very similar for each remaining member of the household. The children participating in this study who came from families in which the father had unexpectedly decided on divorce, described their reactions in the period following the separation in much the same manner as their mothers talked of their own experience. Moreover, the children viewed their mother as sharing their loss and developed a certain closeness with her because of this. This closeness was apparent during the interview in their tendency to talk in terms of what "we" were feeling rather than regarding each individual totally separately.

> *If we were ever going to start over we had to be able to communicate with each other.*
>
> *... mad at him for what he's been doing to us.*

The children seemed to understand what she was going through and were sympathetic with her difficulties.

> *They would just have to ... understand that it's a new thing for the mother and they have to understand she's going to have different moods and feel different at different times.*

However, these children also witnessed a mother who in many cases was severely depressed and was generally less in control of her life. This was clearly frightening for a child whose world had already been made less secure by the departure of one parent.

> *Kind of scared and wondering why is she upset. What is she going to do when she's upset? Because they know what they feel and what they do but their mom is a different person and they never really see her upset so they wonder what she's going to do.*

Additionally, in several instances, the mothers who were having a great deal of difficulty adjusting to the idea of the divorce were reportedly temporarily less emotionally available to attend to the needs of the children.

> *I feel like I kind of ignored mine. I was so busy trying to cope with the job and everything else that maybe I should have listened to them more with what they had to say about it. And if they did bring it up, I tended to change the subject because it was too painful for me to talk*

about. . . . Like my whole world was falling apart and I just went through the motions. There were days when I wasn't really even there with them, you know, emotionally.

Often the children appeared to end up mothering the mother as much as they themselves were mothered. For example one ten and one-half-year-old girl described her mother's reactions to the husband leaving and the changed family situation as follows:

She doesn't talk a lot and sometimes when she's like, when she starts dropping things or feeling dizzy or something and sometimes she has bad nerves and when she gets nervous she's either dizzy or has headaches or stomachaches or something. . . . Well at dinner she usually says like, she hardly ever says anything at dinner and I don't see her after school. She usually says how was your day today or something and I would ask her how was her day and she would say I'm tired and then she would just go lay down on the couch. . . . Before she'd talk about more things like she would say what did you do in Math, what did you do in Reading and then after the dishes, when we didn't have the divorce and Daddy was at work, when she was done with the dishes I'd always ask her if she'd play a game and she'd say I'll play one game with you. And she'd play one game but now she doesn't have any time to play any games. [Now] sometimes I cook dinner, like if it's in a can or something and she's laying down, then I surprised her when she woke up. And then she ate and see, now I usually clean the house up more.

It seems likely that this mutual support giving has a beneficial outcome in that everyone feels they are needed by the other but it may force the child into a position that he/she is too immature to handle. Finally, the children's own upset about the divorce is heightened by their mother's continually unhappy mood.

I felt sad too because when I see her cry then it makes me feel bad inside.

Although the mothers who planned for a divorce still experienced considerable internal turmoil following the separation, the less overwhelming nature of their loss allowed them to hide a great deal from the children. Therefore, with the exception of a few sensitive and highly empathic children, the children were less attuned (than the children referred to in the preceding paragraph) to their mother's problems. They tended to depict the mother as adapting easily to the absence of the father and were occasionally resentful of her or felt alone in their grief as a result. However, in contrast to the mothers who were "left," this group was often able to be more attentive to their children's needs at a point when their children were having the most difficult time. Their guilt due to bringing about a situation which caused their children pain in some cases triggered defenses against noticing the degree to which the children were suffering, but they were usually able to be more concerned with the day-to-day activities of their children's lives. During the interviews, these mothers, although relating that they had felt bad about getting a divorce because of the problems which they had expected it to cause for the children, missed many of the negative feelings related to the divorce which the children reported. In contrast to the mothers described earlier however, they spent a considerable amount of time discussing their children's interests, daily routines and their involvement with them. Many women reported that relief from the tension of their marriage allowed them to become much better parents.

Variations in the Sequence of Events Preceding the Divorce

In addition to variations in the manner in which a couple decides on a divorce, differences in the basic process by which this comes about also alter what comprises a family's divorce experience. For the sample studied, it was most common for a couple to separate once, either shortly before filing for a divorce or immediately afterwards, and then remain separated while the legal proceedings unfolded. However, these families still only accounted for about half of those interviewed, that is, 19 out of 40 families. Nine couples separated for a period of from a few months to a year, reconciled and lived together for approximately another year, and then separated for the final time. Another four couples underwent a series of separations, or more accurately, the husband moved out and back home repeatedly before either he decided that he definitely wanted to terminate the marriage or his wife issued an ultimatum. Finally, for eight families, the decision to divorce and the legal filing occurred months before the separation took place. In all but one of these eight cases, the mother initiated the divorce and the father refused to move out. A few women at first hesitated to insist on his departure, believing there was a slight chance that things would change in such a way that the marriage could work. They eventually became adamant about their decision and the separation ensued. The others were firm in their decision from the beginning and worked with their lawyers to force their spouse to leave.

In cases where the divorce was preceded by two distinct separations, the first one acted as a trial run for the mother. Whereas the initial separation may have triggered intense reactions, these abated during the period of reconciliation and never returned to such an extreme degree. The mothers approached the final separation with the assurance that they could survive without their husband and usually with the conviction, lacking previously, that the divorce was the correct move for them.

It was a total surprise to me when he told me he wanted a divorce and I was very unhappy and miserable for a complete week and then couldn't eat and couldn't do anything but think about it. . . . I was lonely and I didn't have any friends to go out with . . . and I was glad when he came back. . . . The second time when we finally got—decided to divorce, I was very glad that he was leaving. . . . I just wanted out, period, and that was it.

Furthermore, many day-to-day changes which typically accompany divorce such as returning to work and meeting other single mothers had already taken place so fewer adjustments had to be made. To some extent, a series of separations and reconciliations affected the women's reactions in the same manner. However, the repeated experience of being rejected by her husband each time she allowed herself to hope the relationship could work took a severe toll on self-esteem and willingness to trust men. These women also appeared to be more masochistic and passive in general, tendencies which carried over into their manner of dealing with the divorce.

For the woman whose husband fails to move out when she first files for a divorce, the period preceding the eventual separation is remembered as a time of great stress. Angry and hurt feelings which were defended against to a large extent before the decision to divorce was made are now consciously present. These are intensified by the daily encounters with one's spouse but are not resolved. Even though some women reported that their husband made a supreme effort to please them with the hope of avoiding a divorce, all felt extreme relief when the separation finally took place. This relief countered many of the stresses normally experienced when the husband leaves.

It just finally came to a boiling point where he couldn't understand my feelings and how I was reacting and I think I just finally told him I wanted a divorce and I wanted him to move out and then he wouldn't move so it was difficult. And once you've made the decision that it has ended and you don't want him here anymore, it's hard to accept the fact that he won't leave. . . . I couldn't handle his presence here. . . . The final separation was the greatest relief I think I've had in years. The fact that all my tensions, actually all my tensions and frustrations were all gone. He was gone and I was like a totally different person. . . . I was just free of all the bad things that had occurred.

Although prospective longitudinal studies are needed to assess accurately the effect of the course of events leading to the divorce, the data from this study suggest that variations in the steps taken to dissolve the marriage impact little on the children's reactions. From the perspective of our data the various events which precede a divorce become quickly blurred in a child's mind so that reactions of children who experienced multiple separations are similar to those of children who only went through one separation. It seems that children react most strongly when it is made clear that the divorce will take place, holding onto the belief that it won't happen until this time. Thus a separation which they believe to be temporary is largely disregarded (as long as regular contact with the father is maintained) as is an explanation given months before the father actually leaves home.

Variations in the Nature of the Spousal Relationship

Another major area of differences between divorcing families is the quality of the spousal relationship prior to and after the divorce. About two-thirds (27 out of 40) of the women interviewed talked of having years of problems in their marriage and described their relationship with their husband as steadily declining. This group can again be subdivided according to two criteria. First, the nature of the relationship decline varied. For many couples, positive feelings were gradually eroded as problems mounted. However, for a surprisingly large number of others, warm loving feelings toward the spouse seemed to coexist with increasingly extreme negative feelings. Second, the manner in which the couples' difficulties were manifested distinguished one family from another. In half of the cases, the mothers explained that hostility was rarely, if ever, directly expressed. Rather the husband and wife became isolated from one another; straightforward communication regarding what was troubling them (or any other emotionally laden topic for that matter) was nonexistent. In the remaining cases, problems were evident in open and frequent verbal, and in some cases physical, battles.

Approximately one-third of the women are not accounted for in the above instances. Three stated that they realize now that they were not happy with their husband but never thought about this prior to the separation. A group of four women said that until the crises which provoked the divorce occurred (typically the husband having an affair) or until the father actually walked out, they thought they had a good marriage. Finally, six women related that they knew of problems in their marriage but never considered a divorce, assuming that the difficulties could be worked out. Many of these 13 women were stunned when their husbands told them they wanted a divorce.

The general way in which a woman describes her preseparation relationship with her husband appears to be linked with the manner in which the divorce is initiated. Women who filed totally of their own accord or as a result of a joint decision with their husband, tended to describe their marriage as steadily deteriorating over a long period of time. Individuals who asked for a divorce because they were provoked to do so by their husband or who did not actively seek a divorce were divided between the steady decline group and the remaining possibilities. The impact of this variable on a family's functioning postseparation when viewed in general terms seems to be similar to that of who initiated the divorce. This appears to be true because of the connection between a woman's view of her marriage and her degree of preparedness for the divorce, the latter being a major component of the earlier described variable as well.

The more detailed characterizations of the preseparation marital relationship appear to be considerably less important in understanding the individual and family reactions to the divorce. The primary effect of variations in the nature of the relationship decline is on the interactions between the husband and wife during and after the divorce process. The women who continued to feel strongly about their husbands up to the separation tended to remain more emotionally involved with them following the divorce. Either hostile or loving feelings predominated but in both cases the man's behavior (e.g., his social life, his attitude during a phone call) continued strongly to affect the woman's moods on a regular basis. Women who reported that they had little feeling of any sort for their husband, other than some degree of concern, by the time the separation took place, found it much easier to deal matter of factly with the divorce or at least to keep arguments about the settlement at a minimum. This lesser emotional entanglement could usually be maintained after the legal proceedings were completed. The impact on the children of their parents' relationship after the divorce will be discussed later in this chapter.

The issue of whether or not the husband and wife fought openly prior to the separation has remarkably little effect on either the mother or the child postdivorce. The relief experienced by a majority of the mothers interviewed does not appear to be contingent on the degree of directly expressed hostility preceding the separation. Similarly, the children's opposition to the divorce is not described as less intense in families where fighting was commonplace. This finding confirms a similar observation made by Wallerstein and Kelly (1980). Most often children in the age group studied accepted their parents' relationship without questioning its quality or doubting its endurance, and either failed to notice or defensively denied all but the most extreme signs of trouble. The mothers however, frequently asserted that their children were sensitive to the tension in the family and negatively affected by it. This seems likely, although the children were rarely sophisticated enough to talk about it as well as defensively resistant to exploring this issue during the interview. This does not mean that the children connected the tension with the possibility of divorce. Children sometimes mentioned how their parents' fights led to the divorce and at times talked of how bad the fights were. Yet, when their comments were probed, it commonly appeared that this explanation was developed after the events were over, not predicted in advance. Moreover, it often turned out that the children were concretely grabbing onto the one fight they witnessed as the reason for the divorce, a fight which may have occurred between a basically noncommunicative couple. Even when the hostility was extreme and expressed directly and the children were therefore less surprised and shocked by the news of an impending divorce, they rarely shared the mother's opinion that divorce was the best solution. A few said they were glad that their parents no longer lived together. Most shared the desire of children whose parents did not battle openly that the parents reunite.

Westman (1970) looked at the parental relationship postdivorce with regard to whether a continuing or renewed court battle existed between the parents. He regarded the segment of the divorced population who returned to court repeatedly (i.e., 31 percent) as those individuals "who did not terminate the conflictual interaction" which preceded the divorce and assumed that for most of the remaining couples "the divorce was followed either by complete separation of the couple or by a mutually satisfactory resolution of financial and child care arrangements" (p. 417). The picture which emerges is an oversimplified one. First, based on the current sample, the presence of absence or a legal contest postdivorce was not an accurate indicator of the degree of "turbulence" between a couple. The expression of many of the worst conflicts over money, visitation, or custody was limited to threats which never reached court. Moreover, several mothers who would have liked to make changes concerning child support did not even contact their lawyer as they had no confidence in the court's power to enforce any of its decisions. On the other hand, couples who returned to court because of problems with child support payments often had only minor conflicts in other areas. No couple in this study, as compared with approximately 14 percent in Westman's sample, became involved in legal custody or visitation disputes after the divorce process was completed. This is not to say that none had problems in this area.[3] Second, the range of possible relationships between ex-spouses and the nature or cause of conflictual interactions after the divorce is finalized are only touched upon when one focuses on the presence or absence of a court battle.

Mothers' descriptions of their relationship with their ex-spouse since the divorce can, for the most part, be delineated into five mutually exclusive categories:

1. no direct contact at all;
2. feel interactions whether in person or on the phone are strained;

3. able to avoid bitterness and encourage positive father-child relationships, her own feelings are minimal either way or simply friendly;
4. able to avoid bitterness and encourage positive father-child relationships but some anger or tension during contacts is clearly present;
5. still in love and considering a reconciliation.

Six women had no direct contact with their husbands due to their own choosing. All visitation arrangements were made directly with the children, who usually waited outside or at the door for their father to get them. Sometimes the children served as messengers when one parent needed to convey something to the other. During the course of the interview, all of these women revealed a great deal of anger close to the surface. It is important to note that a few of these women did not volunteer that they were angry at first but gradually let their true feelings be known. Sometimes the interviewer mentioning the possibility of anger seemed to give them permission to discuss this.

Eight women emphasized the tension which they experienced when they saw or spoke with their ex-husbands. They talked of how they were still easily upset or angered by the other so that their mood on a given day depended greatly on whether or not they had contact with their ex-spouse. What distinguishes this group from the two to follow is that these women recognized that their negative feelings interfered with comfortable acceptance of a positive father-child relationship. The mother's difficulty in accepting the child's loving feelings toward the father was clearly picked up by the children.

I: If your mom had to choose two things which she wished that you didn't feel about the divorce or your dad, what would they be?
C: *Well, like after not seeing him for a month and he goes out and buys us something, she would wish I never felt good or something.*

Several of these mothers resented the father's ability to devote visitation days solely to the children while they must split their days between work, housework, and the kids. They feared that the children would prefer their father because of this and saw themselves constantly in a losing competition with him.

Eleven mothers had reached a point where they reportedly could interact with their ex-husbands in either an unemotional or a friendly way. The continuing love of the children for the father was supported and efforts were made to have visiting proceed smoothly. Several of these mothers maintained contact with the father around issues concerning the children. For instance, if the mother was informed of a problem at school or if she felt that the child was having difficulty with some aspect of the divorce, she would discuss this with the father. In five instances, father visitation was occasionally treated as a family event. This group includes families in which the father remained or became active in the children's lives and those in which his involvement was limited to sporadic visits. One mother illustrated her feelings toward her ex-husband by responding to the question "What could someone do to make the divorce a lot better?" with the following remarks:

> *Well, you better start talking to each other. . . . I think with little children you just have to. I called Dan right away because he hadn't been around for two weeks and I said you better get over here and talk to Mike because he was just really, he came over and he talked and it made them feel better because they had felt quite deserted. But just, you hear about kids being left on the doorstep or whatever. I don't know. You better keep something open there. I try to still give him quite a bit of responsibility for the kids. They're still his and I need a break once in awhile.*

The next group, consisting of eight women, is similar to the one above in all ways except that anger towards the ex-spouse or some degree of discomfort associated with interactions with him was evident during the interviews. These mothers, however, unlike the second group, seemed able to separate their feelings for the father from their feelings about their children's relationship with him. They valued the father having an ongoing and positive relationship with the children and often mentioned that despite problems in the marital relationship, their ex-husband was always a good father. Much of their anger focused on aspects of the father's present behavior which they felt hurt the children. The two most common examples were anger at his failure to keep regular appointments with the children, especially if he disappointed them by cancelling at the last minute, and at his treating all visits as holidays, showering them with presents, expensive outings or junk foods. Although the latter may also be mixed with some jealousy, the mother's primary reaction is hope that the father-child relationship will become better balanced. Anger may also stem from unresolved issues related to the reasons for the divorce or problems resulting from the settlement (e.g., current financial strain).

Four women indicated that they thought positively about remarrying at the time of the interview. Three of these mothers, in addition to sharing many of the father-child visits, were again involved in a dating relationship with their ex-husbands.

The quality of the ex-spousal relationship postdivorce is associated with the mother's comfort with and degree of resolve about the divorce as a whole. Women who felt relatively little for their husband or who were able to interact with him in a pleasant, nonconflictual (but not loving) way were much more likely to describe themselves as happier and more content with their current situation. Feelings about the divorce or their ex-husbands were not predominant in their lives at this time. These variables are not linked in a simple one-way causative fashion as the same thing could be said in reverse. Rather they go hand in hand, each affecting the other. In addition, it should be noted that a one to one correlation does not exist. Other aspects of the divorcees experience such as difficulty coping with the burden of being a single mother or feeling lonely (i.e., missing having a steady male companion as opposed to missing one's ex-spouse) may greatly affect her feelings on a day to day basis.

The mother's description of her present feelings about her ex-husband also appear to be connected with her ability to form new long-term relationships. For example, of the 11 mothers who were either remarried, had definite plans to be remarried, or had a live-in boyfriend with whom they were seriously involved, 7 indicated that they were able to avoid any bitterness between themselves and their ex-spouses and to encourage a positive father-child relationship. Only one mother who reported feeling strained when she saw her husband and none who still regularly socialized with their husband when he visited the children were involved in a new serious relationship. This suggests that continued involvement with one's ex-spouse makes it difficult for a woman to invest in a new relationship regardless of whether contacts are negative or positive.

The parents' relationship after the divorce is finalized is a central aspect of the child's divorce experience. A child whose parents are now dating each other must cope with a far different situation than one whose mother gets angry or upset each time she speaks to his father. The impact of these differences is obvious. Children whose parents were clearly still angry at each other and let this affect their attitude toward the child-father relationship tended to be more tense when the subject of their father needed to be broached. Visits with the father were often made difficult by concern about hurting the mother. Conflicts stemming from their parents' inability to get along was evident. When a child recognized that his mother was comfortable in his father's presence and supportive of his loving feelings for that parent, he felt far more at ease in showing these feelings to the mother and in discussing the father in general. However, greater comfort with their parents' behavior did not mean that the major reactions to the divorce were circumvented. These children still expressed a great deal of sadness, anger that the divorce occurred, and a longing for their dad. (The reactions of children to the divorce process are discussed in detail later.) The children also were not uniformly more positive about their mother's handling of the divorce. Many of these mothers, with the intention of supporting the father-child relationship and protecting the children from the harsher aspects of the divorce, hid from the children the major reasons for the divorce. For example, one never mentioned that the father was an alcoholic. These problems were often well hidden from the children during the marriage. The mothers believed, that as a result, the children failed to understand why the divorce was necessary and remained angry at their mother, blaming her for the divorce.

Variations in the Nature of the Mother's Postseparation Heterosexual Relationships

With only one exception, the mother's formation of new heterosexual relationships was another important element in each family's divorce experience. How soon this occurred, how it was handled and how quickly the children needed to contend with the introduction of a stepparent differed from family to family. Eleven women, one-fourth of the sample, began to date within a month or two after the separation. The majority of these women went out with several men during the next year and often were occupied with such engagements more than once a week. Six individuals became involved in a serious exclusive relationship which the mother expected would lead to marriage before the divorce became final. All but one of these women were still committed to this same man at the time of the interview. The remaining mothers (besides the one who had not yet dated anyone) had taken a break, usually for six months to one year, between the ending of their marriage and the start of new relationships.

In terms of the manner in which the mother handled the interface between family life and social life, over half (22 out of the 39 who had some form of dating experience) frequently treated dates as a family event. In other words, the children were introduced to the men early on in the relationship and were included in dates on a regular basis. In contrast, 11 mothers kept their dating relationships separate from their children except on rare occasions. Many managed this by seeing men only when the children were staying with their father. An additional six women allowed dates to become family affairs only as they became serious about the relationship. The children may have known with whom the mother was going out but did not truly get acquainted with the man until she decided that the relationship had long-term potential. No connection was apparent between the mother's attitude toward involving the children in her social life and how soon after the separation she began dating. Finally, 10 percent of the mothers had introduced a new adult into the home (4 mothers had remarried by the time of the interview, 4 more planned to be married in the next few months, and 5 had a live-in boyfriend).[4]

The mother's dating impacts on a family's functioning during and after a divorce in several ways. It is important in terms of the role it plays in the mother's resolution of the divorce, the time factor involved, and how it determines who is treated as part of the family unit at any given time. Dating represents more than a divorcee's ability to invest herself in a new relationship. It provides a source for obtaining support around divorce-related issues, particularly as many of the men have been in a similar situation themselves. It also serves to rebuild the woman's self-esteem by assuring her that she is still lovable, attractive, and sexually desirable. Third, it aids the individual in sorting out her part in the marital conflict by giving her the opportunity to see how she relates to other men. She is helped to trust men again and to learn that problems with her husband do not necessarily apply to men in general. Furthermore, it gives her a break from the children and her other responsibilities so that she can relax and recoup. Because of the benefits, the women who began dating immediately usually felt positive about themselves and the divorce quicker than the women who delayed in resuming a social life. However, these advantages were not necessarily permanent. For some women, the rapid investment in new relationships did not appear to represent healthy involvement but rather defensive avoidance of feelings evoked by the divorce. It seemed likely that in these cases, the reactions to the divorce would merely be delayed, or problems similar to those in the marriage would be manifested again. This process was especially evident in one case where a woman stated that she found the divorce process easy emotionally as she quickly found a boyfriend but became exceedingly depressed (e.g., she couldn't eat or work) over six months later when she first saw her husband with another woman. The new relationships of several other women could be characterized as displaced involvement. These women appeared to substitute another man for their husband and, in that way, postponed truly dealing with their loss. They reported being more hurt when the first man they dated broke off with them than by their husband even though these relationships were short-term and the man never indicated he was interested in a long-term commitment.

The women who waited a period of time before beginning to date were less likely to use dating in a defensive manner but were far more isolated in coping with the divorce. Some women viewed this time positively as one of introspection, during which they closely examined what had gone wrong in the marriage and attempted to analyze their contributions to the conflict. They began dating at a point when they felt they could comfortably put the marital relationship behind them. Others were simply too depressed to reach out to someone for help or to get some relief from thinking about the divorce. Commonly, these mothers, when asked what someone could do to make the divorce better, stressed the importance of going out. They felt that they made coping with the divorce more difficult for themselves by remaining so alone.

When this second group of mothers (i.e., those who took a break before dating) began going out they typically became involved with only one person and developed a rather steady relationship. The majority were still seeing the first man they dated at the time of the interview.

The time which a mother devotes to dating entails time she spends away from her children or time in which the children are exposed to new men. While a mother who dates frequently immediately following the separation may be greatly helped by this attention to herself, the children lose out on attention at a point when they are quite needy. They may respond with fear of losing the mother, resentment of her desire to go out, and loneliness. This was often directly reported by the mothers and confirmed by the children. The children reacted in various ways to the mother's attempts to form an independent social life after she had remained primarily at home for a period of time. One main influence on the children's feelings seemed to be how unhappy the mother had been, or more accurately, how much this had been communicated to them. Children were often pleased that their mother had begun dating when she had been very unhappy and dating raised her spirits.

The interaction of the many variables addressed in this chapter is again underlined when one examines the topic of remarriage. A look at the history of the women who are now remarried, living with a man, or are in the process of planning a marriage, reveals additional evidence of the slower adjustment of those women whose husbands unilaterally initiated the divorce. None of the women "left" by their husband is included in this group moving directly toward remarriage.[5]

Variations in Changes Regarding Mothers' Employment

In addition to the shift from a married to a single person's social life, the frequent change in the mother's work status constitutes a large component of the divorce experience to which the family must adapt. Fourteen women began working outside the home during the divorce process or soon afterwards. Three others sought employment during their first separation and then continued working during their reconciliation with their husband and the subsequent divorce. While the majority of these mothers had been employed at some point in their marriage, almost all had worked for just a short period following their wedding until they became pregnant with their first child. Their jobs did not typically represent a career beginning but rather a way to keep busy and earn some extra money for the family. These women had therefore never juggled the time and energy demands of both children and a job nor did they have a clear-cut place in the job market. They viewed themselves as traditional housewives and mothers. Of the women who were working at the time the separation took place, eight had returned to work only shortly before filing for the divorce and did so as one aspect of their preparation for it. Some individuals consciously connected their job seeking and their plans for a divorce; others realized the two were linked as the separation approached. One mother, now employed full-time, described the latter case as follows:

> M: *I hadn't worked in a long time although I had gone back to work part-time a year before he left.*
> I: Was that in terms of thinking that the divorce was going to happen?
> M: *Well, I guess I could say as a gut reaction, that yes, I could see the handwriting on the wall. I mean, it wasn't something that we had planned and we certainly didn't have anything in the works, but I could feel that there was something there that wasn't right, so I assumed that at some point it was going to happen. So therefore, I guess I was subconsciously trying to plan for it.*

Four mothers switched from a part-time to a full-time position while the divorce was underway. Only nine mothers had worked full-time before the divorce became an issue: they all maintained this schedule after the divorce was finalized. Of the remaining two mothers in the sample, one had always worked part-time and continued to do so; one never worked and began receiving ADC.[6]

Family functioning in the immediate aftermath of a separation and divorce is strongly affected by the extent of change in the mother's work status. A full-time job requires that the mother be away from home for at least a few nonschool hours. Since a babysitter was usually too expensive, most mothers in the present sample either sent the children to some sort of day-care center or allowed the children to come home alone. Furthermore, the tasks which the mother had formerly accomplished while the children were at school now needed to be done in the evening or on weekends. The children, who were already spending less time with their mother therefore needed to share her attention in ways not previously necessary. All this was true at the same time that the mother reportedly had less energy, at least when her job was still new, to deal with either the children or the house. Because of the greater demands on her time and her greater fatigue in the evenings, the mothers who were employed full-time often relaxed the strict routines to which they had adhered when they were housewives. For example, dinners often became casual and last-minute affairs. Moreover, the children were requested to share more of the household responsibilities.

Although the above situation is characteristic for all working mothers, women who return to work because of a divorce are making these radical changes in lifestyle at the same time as everyone is dealing with the marital separation. The children therefore need to cope with the reduced availability of the mother at the same time they are adjusting to the lessened availability of the father. The children's interviews revealed that loneliness, loss of a sense of security, and feelings of rejection were heightened as a result. The mothers, on the other hand, felt exceedingly drained, and frequently guilty for the reduction in time spent with their children. Financial worries and fear that they would not succeed at their jobs added to their concerns. The capacity to adapt flexibly to change was thus sharply reduced for everyone. As Wallerstein and Kelly (1980) noted, high tension and hectic pressure become a part of the child-parent relationship as a result.

I found that a regular job was a lot more demanding and I started out at 10 hours a day, six days a week. And when you're not used to working, those hours are something else and I'd come home exhausted.... It bothers them because we don't have our special times like we used to have. We had more time to do things with each other and now it seems like our time is so limited.... It's a hurried-up kind of situation. It's not like it used to be.... A lot of times I'll come home and things will be a disaster area and so the first thing I do when I hit the door is, oh gee, who did this? Who walked all over the carpeting with muddy shoes on, and I start hollering. So I come home from work and they haven't seen me all day and the first thing I do is start hollering. I wouldn't mean to do it or really ever think about it at the time but it got to be the only time we were seeing each other we're hollering about something or they're complaining about something else and this has been our relationship.

Women who worked prior to the divorce, in addition to mastering the dual demands of family and work prior to confronting a divorce, have an already established support system to help them deal with the problems they may encounter. Because the female work force is made up of a high percentage of single, often divorced, women, these mothers have ready access to others in similar situations. Many individuals commented that while they felt more distant from other married friends with whom they had socialized together with their husband, friendships at work became stronger. Their self-esteem, already higher because of their proven ability to function independently, was thus given an extra boost.

Variations in Father Visitation Arrangements

A final area of change for families, unique to the divorce situation, is the establishment of a relationship between the children and a noncustodial parent. As with the other topics discussed in this chapter, families do not structure the visitation relationship in a uniform way.[7] At the time of the interview, no father in this sample had lost complete contact with his children but a considerable range in the frequency of visits existed. As is illustrated in table 1, slightly more than half the families maintained a fairly regular schedule of father-children get-togethers. In seven cases, the children saw their father two or more times a week. Some children lived near their father and had access to him whenever they desired. Six families arranged for the children to see their father on a once a week basis for all or part of a day. Occasionally, these children remained with their father overnight but this was not typically the case. Four sets of children visited with their father each weekend, remaining overnight at his home either Friday or Saturday evening. In five more instances, visits were scheduled for every other weekend. These often included overnight stays but not always. The remaining 18 families had no definite visitation arrangements. In some cases, get-togethers were set up only when the mother called her ex-husband and urged him to see the children. More commonly, the mother made no effort to contact the father and the scheduling of visits were dependent on his whim. Four fathers lived out of town and visits took place on school vacations or when they came to Washtenaw County to see the children. For the other 14 families, visits usually ranged in frequency from once a week to once a month, tending toward the latter. In all of these cases, longer gaps between visits, sometimes for several months, had occurred.[8]

The frequency of father-children visits had remained constant for most of the families since the separation took place. However, in six cases the current number of visits per month represented an increase from the time when the father first left the house. Commonly, these fathers had found it difficult at first to switch from being a full-time to a part-time father, and temporarily decided that if they could not see the children every day they would rather not see them at all. Others realized for the first time during the separation how important the children were to them and made an effort to become more involved with them than they had been even during the marriage. This was true for several of the fathers who consistently saw the children frequently as well. Six fathers saw the children less often now than they had when they first separated. In four of these six cases this was due to the fact that they had moved out of town within the last several months.

In examining the interaction between the mother's reactions to the divorce and the nature of the visitation arrangement, a strikingly strong relationship between a poor postdivorce relationship and irregular visitation is demonstrated. Of the mothers who had no direct contact with their ex-husband, three out of six were members of families with irregular (and consequently infrequent) visitation. All of those mothers who described their present relationship with their ex-spouse as strained (i.e., eight additional mothers) were included in the families with irregular visitation category. Assuming that a simple one-way causative relationship between these

Table 1.   Visitation Schedules

Nature of Visitation Arrangement	Frequency of Visits	Number of Families N = 40
Regular Schedule	2 or more visits each week	7 (17.5%)
	1 visit each week no overnight stay	6 (15%)
	1 visit each week with overnight stay	4 (10%)
	1 visit every other week	5 (12.5%)
Irregular Schedule	Sporadic visits from father who lived out of town, typically included school vacations	4 (10%)
	Totally unpredictable gaps between visits ranging from 1 week to more than a month	14 (35%)

variables does not exist, several observations can be made. First, regular visitation, and the benefits to the children which this entails, seem to be dependent on a working relationship between the spouses. Tensions between the parents are thus apparently rarely separated from parental behavior towards the children. A mother who remains conflicted in her feelings for her ex-husband may interfere with or sabotage his efforts to become more involved with the children or a father who feels similarly with regards to the mother may withdraw from the children to avoid hostile interactions with his ex-wife. It is also possible that some fathers refuse to commit themselves to a visitation routine exactly because this makes life more difficult for the mother. Everyone seems to suffer as a result. Conversely, it seems that failure on the part of the father to establish a definite visitation schedule is the cause of considerable anger and upset for the mother. Her anger seems to stem in part from her concern about her children's disappointment and hurt when gaps between visits exceed a couple of weeks or promised visits fail to materialize. Additionally, a mother may resent the father for failing to share in childcare responsibilities, thus increasing the burden of being a single parent. The mother who learns of the father's intentions to meet with the children only a few days before this occurs and has learned from experience that he may cancel at the last minute is unable to gain much benefit from these visits. Unlike mothers who can count on having a specific day or two off each week or every other week, she cannot plan her life so that her time with the children is less hectic or her time away from them is designed to release tension and provide pleasure. For example, mothers who know that they do not have to take care of the children nonstop, tend to be more patient with their demands. Likewise, since errands and some household tasks can easily be postponed until the children are with their father, weekday evenings are left more open for relaxed family interactions.

Mothers are also indirectly affected by differences in visitation schedules because of their effect on the children's behavior following time with their father. These data indicate that children who see their father often and know for certain that they will see him again within a few days, take the visits more in stride than children who see their father on an irregular basis. There are far fewer reports in the mother interviews of such children coming home from a day with their father very wound up or easily upset and angered. Not surprisingly, visitation is less tension provoking for the mother in these cases. She consequently feels more positively toward the children seeing their father and encourages visits, thereby maintaining this beneficial cycle.

Whereas in most cases, the absence of the father from the home is thought of primarily as a loss for the child, this situation is altered in families where the father demonstrated pathological behavior. The current interviews were not designed to assess degree of psychological disturbance for any family member but certain indications of problems were sometimes quite apparent. Women stated that their ex-husband was an alcoholic or excessively heavy drinker in seven cases and physically abusive of either them or the children in five cases. One father was included in both groups. The parental separation in these families thus signifies that a disturbed parent is no longer a daily presence in the children's lives.

Wallerstein and Kelly (1980) briefly discussed this issue as well. They found, contrary to their expectations, that the nature of the predivorce father-child relationship did not influence the intensity of the child's reactions to the divorce. "The intense longing for the father and the sadness precipitated by his departure occurred among youngsters whose prior experience with the father ranged from abusive and critically rejecting to warm and consistently caring" (p. 53). Although my findings did not contradict this particular observation, they did suggest a different overall picture than the one implied by Wallerstein and Kelly. Children whose fathers were alcoholics or abusive did miss their father a great deal and experienced sorrow because of his absence but their general feelings regarding the divorce did not appear to be as completely negative as was typically the case for children when separated from their father. Mothers and children both related to the extent that the children were aware of the father's behavior (it was well hidden from the children in a couple of cases) they were angered and frightened by it. Several children while not agreeing that they were relieved by the divorce, were relieved that they no longer had to witness the father's difficulties. They were among the few children to be able to supply an answer to the question "What things might get nicer after the divorce?" When the father's behavior had been directed toward the children, their reactions were more severe. In each instance, considerable ambivalence toward the father was evident. Alongside more positive feelings, the children related that they were partly glad their father was no longer living with them and more relaxed now than before the divorce had taken place. Mothers of these children stated the same feelings more strongly.

The factors chosen for discussion in this chapter were selected because they represented major aspects of the divorce situation and clearly divided the sample into contrasting groups. The large range of experiences and their impact on individual and family reactions to the divorce is especially striking because an effort was made to define and narrow the population studied. The participants in this project were limited to families who had experienced a divorce within the last one-half to one and one-half years, had been separated less than one-and-one-half years prior to the divorce, had custody awarded to the mother, predivorce income exceeded $14,000, had two children at least one of whom was between the ages of seven and thirteen years and for whom the divorce was the first divorce for both parents. However, this still was far from a homogenous sample. The differences between families which have been shown to affect family functioning during and after a divorce need to be kept in mind by researchers and clinicians as the mothers' and children's reactions are discussed in more detail.

3

The Mothers' Responses

This is the first in a series of four chapters dealing with the responses of individual family members to the divorce process, as described by themselves and each other. The chapters are organized according to the major areas of reactions noted by the mothers and children. They follow a parallel format to aid the reader in making comparisons, that is, between the reactions of mothers and children, and between the way in which an individual sees him/herself and how he/she is seen by other family members. The interrelationship of the various individuals' reactions will become the central focus of study later.

Because of the different perspectives toward the divorce process with which the mothers approached this project, their descriptions of their reactions ranged from a largely retrospective account to an elaboration of current issues. Most however, did not seem to have truly achieved emotional distance from the divorce. The majority of women (57.5 percent of the 40 mothers interviewed) appeared to the interviewer to still be in he process of reaching a new equilibrium for themselves and their families (that is, a sense of overwhelming crisis had passed but the mothers were not yet comfortable with their postdivorce lives). These mothers presented themselves as having resolved many of their divorce-related feelings but indicated that they were still dealing actively with several issues. Certain feelings originating around the time of the separation, such as loneliness and anger toward their husband, still clearly existed although they were reportedly now experienced less intensely and/or more intermittently. In some cases, strong feelings about their ex-spouse were easily evoked despite involvement in a new serious relationship. Often a mother's recently achieved sense of stability seemed contingent on the continuation of a new relationship. A breakup with a boyfriend threatened her recovery from the divorce. A small number of women (15 percent) remained engrossed with the divorce and/or their ex-husband. They described their feelings primarily in the present tense.

According to the impressions of the interviewer, only 11 women (27.5 percent) were content with their present living situation and had settled into a reorganized life pattern.[1] These mothers almost always discussed their reactions to the divorce in the past tense. While this last group of women did not demonstrate any difficulty vividly recalling the various phases of their divorce experience, their relative lack of current involvement with the issues discussed makes it more difficult to detect where their memory had been affected by defensive distortions.

For all the mothers, the interviews reflected a mixture of practical and emotional concerns. It proved impossible to explore the psychological ramifications of a parental separation without discussing the practical features of divorce as well. Each impacted on the other so that the women were unable to completely separate the two in their responses.

Depression

> *There is nothing good about going through a divorce. It is physically, mentally, and emotionally, at least for me and for the people that I know that have gone through one, exhausting. It's just, regardless of your feelings for the person who you're divorcing, I just, I don't think it can be made easier. It is not a fun thing to go through. . . . I suppose if you realize that it's going to be a very painful process, you won't be surprised when you get into it.*

The mother who made the above statement initiated her divorce and related no regrets about its occurrence. Furthermore, she is one of the 11 women who were regarded as having successfully completed the transition from wife and married mother to single parent. Her negative view of divorce therefore underlines the magnitude of this crisis and the near universality of painful feelings associated with it. Despite the increasing frequency of divorce in this country, almost everyone interviewed emphasized how seriously they viewed the commitment of marriage and/or the decision to divorce. ("I simply come from a Protestant middle-class home where marriage just is. . . . When you marry someone, it is forever." "I'm a Catholic, so it was something that I had never considered in my realm of experience." "I'm from the South . . . and when you get married, you're married. You don't get a divorce. It's for better and for worse and I think that's what you think for a long time.")

Thirty-five of the 40 mothers interviewed spontaneously referred to feeling depressed for at least a brief period after the divorce process had begun (i.e., after the legal filing or the separation had taken place). Typically, these women used the word "depression" as synonymous with sadness or emotional pain. An examination of the mothers' reports however, frequently reveals a clinical picture of depression as well. This depression is characterized by a sense of being overwhelmed by stress accompanied by a feeling of low self-esteem.

The mothers described themselves as immobilized by their pain. Daily routines such as cooking and cleaning were seen as enormous burdens and requiring more energy than could usually be mustered. In a few severe cases, the women were unable to get out of bed in order to go to work. Child care was commonly reduced to basic routines and provided little satisfaction. Six mothers related that they found themselves unable to eat and lost a great deal of weight. In general, the women's ego seemed paralyzed, leaving them unable to cope with the loss of their marriage. They became almost totally self-absorbed but were ineffectual in gaining control over their intense feelings.

> *It was probably the most emotionally wrenching time. I totally accepted it to the point you could, however, I would guess my emotions had never been torn apart in my whole life. . . . I basically had to sit around and suck my thumb, drank too much, and was very down. It was just a time of extreme effort just to exist. You just can't. I just couldn't pull myself out of my own feelings, the mish-mash, the confusion of all those feelings. A very sad time, a very, very sad time. Like I said, your emotions are on edge. You have very little to give to anyone else. You're just almost consumed yourself with the whole thing. So I pretty kind of, much kind of shut down as a human being for a long time.*

(The woman quoted was referring to the six-month period beginning with her separation.)

In an effort to explain their difficulty coping, 11 mothers related that they felt as if their world had been turned upside down. They had never anticipated being divorced and felt lost now that the future they had counted on no longer existed.

> *It was just awful. I felt like, I mean I could see now that I was a baby in a cradle and somebody had yanked the blanket off or something. Like just the whole world was pulled out from underneath me.*

Twelve other women spoke of their sense of emptiness. They stated that their life seemed meaningless without a spouse. While this feeling in part resulted from the loss of a significant object, it also was understood by the mothers as stemming from the loss of a role which made them feel useful. Without the guidelines dictated by their definition of "wife" such as looking good for their husband and having a hot meal on the table when he returned from work, they felt they were floundering. In seven cases, this sense of upheaval and/or emptiness was so profound that the mothers seriously contemplated or (in three instances) attempted suicide by taking an overdose of drugs.

The low self-esteem of the recently separated woman was reflected in her description of herself as worthless and/or unlovable. Thirty women (12 spontaneously, 18 in response to a direct question) readily elaborated their belief that "something must be wrong with me or I wouldn't be divorced."

Some mothers generalized these feelings to include all aspects of their personality. They found the divorce a totally degrading experience and subsequently regarded themselves as bad people.

For a long time I felt like I was walking around with a sign that just flashed out: divorced, unwanted, deserted, abandoned, no good, don't touch.

I'm just not worth a hill of beans.

Eight women specifically labeled themselves a failure. They regarded the divorce as a defeat in their efforts to have a successful marriage. The fact of the divorce labeled them a loser.

I felt like a total and complete failure. . . . It was just, how can you do such a thing? Why couldn't you work it out? I felt that I had failed myself and my children and my marriage and everything I had been taught to expect out of life was a lie and I just felt that I had totally and completely failed in my obligations as a wife and a mother and a person.

(The guilt feelings which are also evident in the above reaction will be examined later.)

Most commonly, the focus of the women's self-derogation was that they were unlovable. They doubted their ability to sustain a relationship with someone. If they initiated the divorce, their thoughts usually took the form of "something is wrong with me or the marriage would have lasted." If the husband initiated the divorce or prompted it by having an affair, their thoughts more often took the form of "something is wrong with me or he wouldn't have stopped loving me." Both groups assumed that they were inadequate in some undefined way and thus incapable of making anyone happy.

The mothers also doubted their own desirability. They described feeling ugly or sexually unattractive. Even though they were able to enumerate the reasons why the divorce occurred, they could not abandon the thought that if they were somehow prettier or sexier their husband would not have left. They believed that nobody would ever want them again. These feelings seemed more acute for those women whose husbands had become involved with other women, either during the marriage or after requesting a divorce. The mothers' sense of worthlessness seemed to be given support by what was regarded as their husbands' rejection of them. Nineteen mothers described the intense hurt they felt when their husband unexpectedly pulled away from them. Words like "disowned," "left out," and "replaced" were commonly used during their interview. The lack of understanding of their husband's behavior made it extremely difficult for these women to come to terms with the divorce. "This was probably the hardest part to accept—that he rejected us for someone else, his family and his home and his wife." For many, their pain was increased by what appeared to be deliberate attempts on the part of their husbands to flaunt their new romance. For example, one mother related how her husband brought his girlfriend to a party at his family's house before the separation took place. The children also often intensified their mother's sense of rejection by happily informing their mother of what they did on their visit to dad and his new girlfriend/wife. Some mothers discouraged their children from sharing the events of a visit because it caused all their hurt to resurface.

Loneliness

> *It's something that's still ongoing. It's a different kind of loneliness. It's not, your kids can be here all the time and you can have lots of friends and go places and do things. But it's the kind of loneliness for the special companionship that you had, like a relationship that you had with your husband, you know. It's somebody that's here. Somebody that cares, somebody that loves you, somebody you enjoy being with and doing things with.*

Whereas the depression following a separation seems to be primarily a response to the loss of a husband, loneliness is linked more to the problems of becoming a single parent. Loneliness exacerbates the depressed feelings but occurs because a loving relationship does not exist, not because a specific relationship is missed. Loneliness therefore often persists long after the depression has abated and may actually worsen over time. It is perhaps due to the longevity of the feeling that loneliness was one of the most frequent answers to the question "What would you tell other women as the hardest things they'll have to face?"

Loneliness was characteristically described as longing for adult male company. While a few mothers asserted that the presence of the children eased their loneliness, the majority explained that even though they loved the children, there was a limit to the rapport that one could have with a youngster. Similarly, friendships with other women were a great support but did not really eliminate their sense of being alone.

Being alone as far as not having, okay, my kids are older so I don't have the problem of little tiny kids and having to talk down to them, but you cannot have the same kind of conversation with even teenagers that you can have with an adult, or the companionship. I think that's probably the biggest thing that was hardest for me to adjust to because my husband and I did a lot of things together and I missed having someone to do those things with, not necessarily go out but just having someone there. And not, even having a good friend who is a woman is not anywhere near, at least for me, does not have the same kind of relationship that you have with a man.

The emphasis in many explanations of loneliness was on the fact that once a live-in mate was gone, all contact with other adults required an effort. Even women who stated that they usually enjoyed being alone, consented that it was hard never to have anything just set up—never to have someone simply around during times when they were not otherwise committed.

In addition to the expressed need for male companionship, the loneliness also consisted of a need for physical closeness. Women repeatedly related that they were surprised at the intensity of their desire for sex and to be held in general.

I think the biggest thing is sleeping by yourself. You're used to having a warm body there and then all of a sudden nobody's there anymore and I think the nights are the worst. It's terrible because at least during the day you're busy. But then after the kids go to bed and you're all by yourself, and you sit and watch T.V. I did that for quite a while.

The times which were specifically husband-wife times were regarded as the most difficult. Also hard were those instances in which another adult would have been very helpful.

There have only been a few times when I've really felt lonely. I don't know as far as, well when you have a problem with the children and you don't have anybody else to talk to about it, even though he wasn't there anyway and the state of mind he might have been in at the time you wanted to talk to him about it, there's still nobody there to talk about it to that can relate to your child with you.

Problems with the house provoked similar feelings.

Sense of Isolation

Some of your friends you don't see anymore because they're married and you're not anymore so you just don't fit in. It's hard to get out and meet new friends and start building a new life again.

Although it was commonly stated that the best way to cope with the depression and the loneliness would be to socialize and seek support from peers, 30 of the 40 women said that they felt isolated from their friends following the separation. This isolation can be quite profound in that it is fostered both by the former network of friends and the woman herself. Prior to the separation the interviewees' social life was typically dominated by activities with other couples. With the advent of the divorce process, these relationships changed. Even in cases where other wives made an effort to continue friendships with divorced mothers, contacts tended to become restricted to daytime get-togethers or conversations during unplanned encounters as in the supermarket. Invitations for couple events on weekends and evenings reportedly ceased. It seems that people feel uncomfortable or do not think to include a single person in a group otherwise consisting of pairs. Thus, at the very times when a divorced mother is most likely to be free and to miss companionship, she is excluded by her friends.

In the view of the women participating in this study, friends also pull back because they are unsure of how to be helpful. Rather than risk saying the wrong thing or being regarded as intrusive, they do nothing. One woman described this situation as follows:

It is fairly true that you lose your married friends and I think for me that was the biggest thing. When you've been close to married friends for ten, twelve years and for them to turn their backs on both of you, I think it's one of the most cruel things that people can do.... That even people in the church when you say we need to be able to support people who are in emotional pain more, like going through a divorce or whatever, they will say well, we don't want to butt in. When people ask us, we'll be glad to help. And my comment is that they can't ask. They're feeling so depressed and so down that they can't say I need help.... I can remember a couple Sundays just being like—I wish somebody would ask us over for dinner.... I thought that just even if another couple had invited the children and myself over, there would have been a draining away of some of the emotional feeling.

Additionally, the mothers often interpreted their friends' withdrawal to be a result of their feeling threatened. Couples appeared to be threatened by the possibility that association with a divorced person would cause trouble in their own marriage; women appeared to be threatened that the divorcees would steal their husband.

> *Your friends are not your friends anymore. The wives of the couples you used to associate with, they're threatened. They actually think you're after their husbands. Like with your neighbors. When I was married, it was nothing—I'd walk over to their house and sit down and talk with their husbands and they thought nothing about it, until I got divorced. And then it's, "What's she doing over here?"*

Finally, the social life which had become merged with an ex-husband's business obligations is suddenly terminated. Women reported seeking out people they considered friends of their own who avoided them because of a loyalty to the ex-husband and/or their own spouse.

Other people however, are not solely responsible for the isolation experienced by a divorced woman. In addition to the difficulty reaching out at a time of stress, many women stated that they purposely withdrew from the people with whom they had been close.

> *I just feel embarrassed in a way, thinking that it actually happened to us, you know, it was sort of, I really didn't want to tell people. It was just sort of degrading I guess you might say.*

> *I didn't feel like going out and I didn't really feel like I was very nice to be around at the time and I didn't feel like I should inflict myself on other people if I was going to be moody and not any fun.*

> *I didn't seek too much in the way of support from my family or friends either. I think if you, in my case maybe it was pride and again maybe it was the fact that I didn't feel comfortable with it, the bad times especially.*

This self-imposed isolation is commonly most severe just before or when the separation takes place. Besides the reasons just mentioned, the women related that they were reluctant to share their problems in case they reconciled with their husbands. They believed that future contacts as couples would be awkward if friends knew about the marital difficulties. Furthermore, they hoped that by failing to reveal their problems they increased the chances of them being worked out. The result of this decision to hide the possibility of divorce was that individuals were likely to be most alone at the exact time when support was needed.

By the time the interviews for this project took place, 17 of the mothers had combatted their isolation by developing a new social network. In large part, these new friends were other divorced mothers. They were met at work, at singles organizations, or at cooperative or condominium complexes where the families moved. (Because of the lower monthly payments required, townhouse developments are often populated by single mothers.) Additionally, casual acquaintances from before the separation who were also recently divorced became closer friends. Even mothers who eventually resumed relationships with some of their predivorce friends, tended to form new friendships with other single parents at this time. The women interviewed stated that they were attracted to other divorced mothers because of shared concerns and perhaps more importantly, shared schedules (e.g., full-time work, weekend days without the children, etc.) and life styles. A divorce therefore commonly results in changes in relationships that extend beyond husband-wife and other family ties.

Anger

There were times when I would have liked to blow him away because of the way I felt, like why did you do this to me, I was a good wife to you. . . . Yes, you do get angry, very angry sometimes.

Anger towards one's husband/ex-husband is an unavoidable part of the divorce process. It was evident in some form for all 40 of the women interviewed. However, despite the fact that anger was more common than any other reaction, the mothers were often uncomfortable acknowledging it. In 13 cases, including the one quoted above, it was not revealed until a specific question was asked. Moreover, in a large portion of the other families, it emerged, at least initially, in a manner that was disguised or displaced. For example, the mother commented that she expected that the children would soon prefer other activities to seeing their dad or the mother railed against her ex-spouse's girlfriend or wife or the people he worked with who encouraged loose morals. In several cases, the mother asserted that she never or no longer felt angry and then later either spoke about her hostility directly or manifested it in the tone of her voice. For instance, one mother who stated early in the interview that her anger towards her husband ceased when the divorce was obtained and was replaced with an acceptance of him "for who he is," later commented, in talking about her son's disappointment with his father, "I couldn't just say you know, your dad's rotten. He's not going to visit. He never did anything with you." A number of women seemed to interpret the interviewer's probing about anger as permission to express this emotion and followed their brief remarks with an outpouring of feeling.

Overall, the most commonly reported cause of anger related to the father's actions involving the children. In keeping with the interviewees' need to have their animosity legitimized, they tended to find it necessary to present it as rational and justified. The children's hurt feelings appeared to be considered by almost everyone to be the best reason for anger. Anger connected to concerns about the children's welfare is also anger which apparently can be shared. The shame, or belief that anger is something which shouldn't be felt, which appears to underlie much of the mothers' discomfort in describing their hostility, was usually absent when the focus was on the children. It is likely that this is true within the mothers' support groups as well.

The complaints about their ex-husbands were varied. Frequently, the mothers found fault with them for disappointing the children by last-minute cancellations of or changes in visitation arrangements. They were angry when the fathers' unavailability caused the children to feel rejected or to miss out on certain experiences like father-son baseball games or fishing outings. This was particularly intense when it was felt that the father paid more attention to his step-children than to his biological children. The mothers also resented their ex-spouse's failure to occasionally convenience visitation times to their schedule so that they could make certain plans without the children. Delays in or incomplete payment of child support checks were another source of anger. Additionally, mothers were infuriated when the fathers challenged their authority with the children. For example, one woman described how her husband purposely put down their religion at the point when she started giving the children religious training. Relatedly, they were furious when the father disparaged them to the children. In some families, name calling seemed to become standard after the divorce. Mothers related that they learned from the children that their fathers referred to them as a slut or whore. Finally, mothers were angry at their ex-husbands when they behaved in ways they considered inappropriate with the children. For instance, they were bothered by his lying to the children (especially when they were expected to back him up) or his allowing girlfriends to sleep over while the children were spending the night.

When anger continued to predominate the mother's feelings for her ex-husband, it was difficult for her to be supportive of the children's positive feelings for their father. The anger was often manifested in her ambivalence regarding any behavior on the part of the children which would create distance between them and their father.

Sometimes I'm glad when they say that they don't want to go out there. That's probably not very nice to say but I am. But then I think that that's being unfair to him. He's still their dad and he deserves to see them. And I want them to see him. But I don't know, it just kind of makes me feel good

when they say they don't want to go. And that's hard for me to deal with
sometimes because I think I shouldn't feel like that, I shouldn't be bitter
or resentful or whatever it is but I am.

Ten women alluded to mixed feelings about their children's love for or anger towards their father. It seems likely that this reaction is even more prevalent but hard for some people to admit.

A final pattern of expressing anger discussed during the interviews is directing hostility toward one of the children when he/she (typically he) acts like the absent parent. This was mentioned by only four mothers, but again probably occurs more frequently. The mothers explained that a large part of their anger stemmed from a fear that the traits their son shared with his father would cause him to mature into a similar unlikeable adult. They realized regretfully however, that at times they were merely "taking out" their anger on their child because he was an available object.

Guilt

I felt guilty because I had failed my children. More than anything else, I
felt they deserved to have a home and be like the other kids and have a
mother and father. The biggest guilt was because of them, that I had
somehow deprived them of what they couldn't help.

The decision to divorce is a complicated one for parents. A large majority of the mothers interviewed eventually concluded, whether or not they believed it to be true at the time of the separation, that pursuing a divorce was a positive move for them. However, many felt far less certain of the benefit for the children. Twenty-five mothers reportedly experienced considerable guilt over the notion that the parents' inability to succeed at marriage should have negative consequences for their offspring.

Certain forms of guilt were typically linked to the mother's having had an active role in seeking the divorce. Most simply, these women stated that they felt guilty for causing their children pain. They related that they felt extremely selfish for what they viewed as improving their situation at the expense of the children's happiness. Relief was experienced when the children appeared relaxed again but guilt threatened to reemerge each time the children developed a problem which would not have existed without the divorce. Many mothers stated that they felt guilty about "taking the kids away from their father." They were both sorry that the children missed their father and the activities that they had shared on a daily basis, and also that they were depriving them of a "male figure" in the home.

Guilt was also connected to the demands of single parenthood. Mothers had guilt feelings about the length of time they needed to be away from their children for the purposes of full-time work and for a social life. Additionally, mothers experienced guilt regarding the quality of the time they spent with the children. The impossibility of keeping up with the "supermom" image perpetuated by the mass media (i.e., having unfailing energy for work, mothering, and men) left many women feeling inadequate.

Sometimes, but considerably less frequently than they were concerned about the children (19 women as compared with 25), the interviewees commented that they felt guilty in relationship to their husband. Particularly (although not exclusively) when the wife initiated the divorce despite the husband's wishes to the contrary, she experienced guilt for pushing him away.

> *Oh, guilt. A lot of guilt. Because I was the one that said this is it and it's over and I knew my husband didn't want to leave. He just hated to leave but he realized at the same time that he really had no choice. And I guess I wouldn't have forced him to but it certainly wasn't working and he knew it wasn't working and something had to be done. I felt very guilty for a long time.*

Allegedly, the husbands could be very manipulative in evoking these feelings by taking every opportunity to let their wife know how unhappy they were.

Fear

> M: *What was my major reaction? The biggest thing I felt? I felt very frightened of the whole thing.*
> I: Can you describe what you were afraid of?
> M: *I was afraid of having to be self-supporting. I was afraid of what society would think of me as a divorced person. I was afraid of not having the sort of womb-like feeling of being safe in a marriage and secure. . . . Also my parents had been divorced too and I had some fears in relation to that.*
> I: Like what?
> M: *I knew how that had affected me and how it had, I think, hampered my growth as a person and how it had affected me in ways and I was afraid of doing that to my children.*

Fear is a central feature of the divorce experience. Almost all the women reported having been afraid of some aspect of their new life; many described their fear as having been pervasive. Fear is one of the first divorce-related emotions to be felt. It accompanies the decision-making process for those who initiate the separation, often delaying definite action for a period of up to several years. It quickly follows shock for those who must deal with a divorce unprepared.

Over half of the interviewees (19 spontaneously, three when asked directly) discussed a generalized fear of the unknown future. The predictability of their lives had been undermined and planning ahead now seemed futile.

Sure there were times when I was absolutely scared to death, you know, uncertainty and not, and I still feel that way. My life is not what I want it to be now and it's uncertain for me and that is, I think for a lot of people, really hard to deal with.

The mothers nervously questioned whether they could cope without a mate, raise the children on their own, face their friends and relatives and, on the whole, deal effectively with their massive responsibilities. The intensity of their emotions at the time of the separation alarmed them. They doubted their own normalcy and feared that the pain would never cease. Their upset, coupled with the overall shakiness of their future also resulted in an exaggerated response to events that previously would have been taken in stride. The women stated that "everything [seemed] just paramount at the time" so that they worried incessantly.

When discussing specific worries, the mothers were most comfortable in dealing with practical issues. Three out of four women detailed their fear that they would be unable to manage on their own financially. Many women described how they spent enormous amounts of time calculating their potential earnings and expenses to make certain they could fare successfully without their husband before going ahead with any divorce actions. One-fourth of the women stated that they had been concerned about their ability to find employment and adjust to working full time.

Well I was afraid, you know, because I wasn't sure how I was going to handle the whole, it suddenly felt like the whole thing was on my shoulders and I hadn't been working since the children were born so it was a whole different life style from what I knew. I couldn't do the things I'd done before and I had to go look for a job.

Seventeen women also discussed their fear of being alone. Particularly at the outset of the divorce process, the mothers were frightened of the loss of security both in an emotional and a physical sense. Primarily, they feared losing an established relationship with a man. They dreaded the loneliness and wondered if they were strong enough to function without leaning on a mate. Many had never known anything but marriage as an adult—they worried about going places alone, making decisions on their own, and maintaining a house by themselves.

While they desired to meet someone new, 26 women commented that they had been leery of men since the divorce. The intensity of this fear ranged from panic to caution but the central concern was the same in all cases; the women were afraid of being hurt again as they were in their marriage. Although they stated that they knew intellectually that their husband was a single individual, they found it difficult not to generalize their negative view of him to all men. They had little faith that a man's love and commitment to them could be lasting.

> *I was really bitter against men, you know, up until now. I still am. I don't think I could ever trust men again. Well you know, if I imagine that I was to remarry I wouldn't trust him as far as fidelity. I wonder if any of them is capable of being faithful. And then on a short-term basis, I wonder what they are after. Like if they ask me out I wonder why—what do they want out of it?*

> *I put so many years into our marriage... what's to be different with another man? It makes you get scary feelings about that.*

Twenty women indicated that their concerns at the time of the separation involved the children. For the most part, their fears fell into two categories. They were afraid of hurting the children and they worried about changes in the children's feelings towards them. With regard to the former, they were concerned initially with simply causing their children any pain. They were torn between their desire to better their own situation and a wish to protect the children from the problems of marital disruption. In thinking of the future, they were frightened that the divorce would negatively affect the children's psychological development, harming their progress in school and their relationships within the family and to other children. Usually their fears were vague and the mothers were relieved when the expected melodramatic reactions failed to appear. Boys were the object of worry more often than girls with the belief that the absence of the father from the home would interfere with the boy's masculinity.

The mothers' concerns about possible changes in the children's feelings for them usually consisted of a fear that the children would blame them for the divorce and be angry as a result. Many mothers panicked when the children were hostile towards them, feeling that their relationship had been permanently impaired. At times this was expressed in terms of a worry that the children would demonstrate a preference to live with their father.

The Pressures of Single Parenthood

I remember the first time I brought out the garbage. I just sat on the steps and cried and I thought, "I just don't have time to take out the garbage. That was something he used to do and here I am, working full time, coming home and cooking dinner, cleaning the house, and trying to spend time with the kids, and how could I possibly have time to take the garbage out."

It has already been discussed how mothers feel psychologically overwhelmed by the intense feelings they experience during the divorce process. Even after this acute reaction to the divorce process has abated, the realistic changes in the woman's living situation continue to create enormous pressures.

The seemingly unending tasks of a single mother can be overwhelming at times. Thirty-three women discussed the pressures which arose because the demands on their time exceeded what was possible in a day. Twenty-seven raised this issue without any prompting from the interviewer. Several factors contributed to their feeling of being overburdened. First of all, the number of responsibilities had increased tremendously following the separation. Many women who had never worked were now needing to combine a full-time job with their previous domestic chores, including the complete care of the children. Every woman needed to attend to the jobs at home which formerly had been accomplished by their husband. Perhaps more important than the actual number of tasks was the lack of relief. Several women commented that even though they did just about everything during the marriage, the situation was still far more difficult now because no back up existed. No one was available to take over in those moments when the woman felt she could no longer cope.

Besides the physical burden, most of the women interviewed found it very hard not to have someone to confer with, to stand behind them, or at least to provide a shoulder to cry on when problems occurred. The other spouse's role as buffer between them and the children when they were angry or frustrated was also missed. The greatest emotional drain was reported to be the shortage of peaceful relaxing time alone.

It never gets to the point where it really stops, where you kind of do that which I consider healthy, and you need that time and I haven't seen it in a long time and that's quiet time.

Sometimes I feel just really that I don't ever have any time to myself because I have the kids all the time and if I don't get a break from them I'm going to go absolutely crazy.

Financial concerns played a part here as well. Working hours could not be shortened to alleviate the general time pressures because of the need for the mother's income. Moreover, the knowledge that her salary might not completely cover the family's costs created anxiety which heightened her tendency to feel overwhelmed.

Because I'm under financial pressures and everything, how am I supposed to make my kids happy, how am I supposed to be happy, you know? This is the whole thing really. And I can't really work enough to make the money that we really need because my kids need me and I have other things that I have to do and I feel that I am spread so thin that sometimes I feel that it's just overwhelming—the things that I'm supposed to be.

A final factor, mentioned by 16 women, contributing to the difficulty of being a single parent is the necessity of altering one's concept of the role of wife/mother. In most of the families studied, marital roles had been stereotypically divided. The divorce thus required the woman to assume responsibilities she had formerly considered to be a man's job. Some found the assumption of these new responsibilities exciting; others cited them as the chief reason for their sense of being overloaded. Even in families where the mother had been working full time prior to the separation, the father usually took care of paying the bills and otherwise managing the money, attending to the upkeep of the house, and maintaining the car.

I had never made any decisions on my own. I wasn't that independent. I had always worked. I was holding a full-time job. But any decision with the house or bills or anything like that, my husband always took care of that.... It's a real hard thing to get used to knowing that you've got to take care of everything in the house, all the repairs, all the work. The car to take care of and the bills and a full-time job and the responsibility of kids, disciplining them and everything. It can really get to you. It's a big burden. It's hard.

Becoming the sole disciplinarian presented an additional problem. While it was not uncommon for the mothers to take part in disciplining the children before the separation, the husband was typically viewed as the final authority. Following the separation, the women attempted to assume the father's position, expecting the children to behave out of a combination of respect and fear. This switch in role was often unsuccessful as the children refused to "mind" [them] like they did their dad."

Most women indicated that they found it impossible to organize their time in such a way that they could juggle all the responsibilities placed upon them. They coped with the overload by reducing their attention to some tasks. Often the first area to be neglected was the domestic chores, one which had occupied much of their time in the past. Some continued to be bothered by the fact that their homes were not as clean or orderly as they had formerly been. Several commented that their prior perspective had been altered now that their daily sphere had widened. They no longer placed such a high value on the appearance of the home. Many however, felt that the children also lost out because of the increased demands on their time. Nineteen women made some reference to a conflict about their reduced capacity to attend to the children's needs. They regretted that their physical and emotional fatigue prevented them from being as good a parent as they wanted to be.

> *Knowing that often you're too tired and too strung out to give to them, to give to any other human being. You just have had it. So it's that feeling of frustration, of not being able to, feeling that you just can't give everything that you need to. . . . There's just not enough of you to go around.*

While the problem of failing to meet all the perceived needs of the children is particularly intense during the divorce process because the reactions described earlier are so draining, it remains an ongoing one. In addition to the times when they cannot attend to the children because of feeling overwhelmed, mothers are often faced with a choice between satisfying their own wants and those of their children. Some mothers related that they stayed home at first whenever the children asked them to as they felt bad and/or guilty about their limited time together. Most eventually decided that it was important for them to rest or enjoy a social life which excluded the children. Yet, the large number of speeches given during the interviews on the topic of meeting one's own needs versus meeting the children's needs, such as the one that follows, reveals the degree of conflict which exists over this issue.

> *I think they need to take care of themselves and particularly women get caught in the whole thing of taking care of the children and taking care of everybody else's needs and putting themselves last. And if they get in that kind of situation, then they aren't going to be able to function and won't be able to do anything for their children and I think, just in general, that's one of the things I see happening in women. They feel they have to meet everybody else's needs first. And I think sometimes they should just sit down and stop and think, wait, I can't meet anybody else's needs until I meet mine. Then I'll be able to give.*

Despite the mothers' love for their children, their distress when they think the children are receiving too little nurturing and their resolve to get away from home for fun sometimes, children could be regarded primarily as a burden. A quarter of the mothers expressed negative feelings, ranging from a complaint that they felt "bogged down" with the children's demands to a description of their resentment of the children's possessiveness. This latter group, although sympathetic at first, soon came to perceive the children's upset or clinginess when they (i.e., the mothers) attempted to go out as manipulative behavior. The women considered it important to communicate that they would not let the children control their life.

Mothering in general is very difficult following a separation. In addition to helping their children with the normal daily problems, mothers in divorcing families must deal with the children's reactions to a major crisis. Coupled with their temporarily reduced capacity for parenting, elaborated earlier, this added responsibility leaves many women feeling "at ends."

> *I felt like I was coping with enough trying to be on my own and take care of them and I really didn't need that extra kind of hassle.*

Fourteen women revealed a mixture of anger and helplessness in response to their children's reactions to the divorce. They felt particularly upset by the children's display of anger, whether it was manifested in generalized "rebelliousness" and tantrums, or directed at them. Also difficult were the children's comments that they wanted to live with their father and their unwillingness to abandon the wish that the parents would get back together again. The mothers found it difficult to control their own anger towards the children and were confused as to how to handle the problem. They usually failed to look beyond a surface explanation of the children's behavior.

> *I didn't know what to do because I tried everything. I tried being stern with him, I tried to be sympathetic with him, and I just felt that nothing was working. I think you get to the point that you don't think you can cope with it.*

Mothers appeared to have far more difficulty dealing with their sons than their daughters. All the specific children mentioned in this regard were boys.

Positive Reactions

> *It was gradual but I liked living so much more by myself and with the children. I started to become the mother that I needed to be much more. . . . I started feeling more like I was relating to them on a new level.*

It's difficult to put into words. I can feel it even now. I can go back and flash back into those feelings. More or less that they were my life and I no longer had to be concerned where Joe had disappeared to for four days and didn't have to worry—all the different creditors calling for bills that he owed and that type of thing. There was tremendous relief to be able to go on and that in combination with just the time and space.

Although there was nearly universal agreement among the interviewees that divorce is both a personal and family crisis, it is initiated in order to remedy a bad situation. Particularly for those women who sought the divorce, the reactions therefore were not altogether negative.

The most frequently mentioned positive response was relief. As stated previously, the decision to divorce is not one that is typically made easily. It is preceded by a long period of internal turmoil. The 16 women who stated that they were relieved when the final separation took place, emphasized how difficult it was to say that they really "wanted out." The burden of the responsibility for this decision, combined with their unhappiness in the marriage caused them a great deal of pain. Once they finally initiated the divorce process (assuming the separation occurred at this point) there was a tremendous relief from tension.

It had been a bad marriage and so by the time we had come to the point where we needed to part it was a real need and when he was gone I was glad.

I think I took so long to make the decision of what I needed to do, that once I had made the decision, it was actually calming to make the decision . . . and once I had made the decision I wanted him to leave right then and there.

When the husband did not leave at once, the tension reportedly escalated and relief was delayed until the separation occurred.

Nine women who did not initiate the divorce still experienced relief when it was finally granted. Although they were unhappy and may have wished to remain married, they found it far easier to cope with their situation knowing it was definite. The unresolved nature of the separation period with its frequent hostile confrontations had been experienced as a severe strain.

Five women described the months following their divorce as a "fun time." Although this group accounts for only 12.5 percent of the sample population for this study, their comments are worthy of note because they present such a contrast to the largely negative reports of the majority of the interviewees. These women reacted to the cessation of tension at the time of the separation with more than relief. Their delight with their newly found "breathing space" spilled over into other aspects of their lives. They enjoyed the opportunity to be by themselves and to choose activities which pleased them. Furthermore, mothering became a pleasurable activity again. The women explained that their unhappiness during the end of the marriage had precluded more than the most basic involvement with the children's activities. Now they had time to spend with the children and the interest to do so. Overall, they characterized the separation and/or postdivorce period as a time of personal growth.

A somewhat larger group of women (11 out of 40 mothers) stated that they saw a positive side to being without their husband now. They elaborated their views in terms of the absence of the negative qualities of married life. For example, the mothers reported that they enjoyed the freedom of not having to be home at a certain time to cook dinner as their husband had expected. They liked the less structured approach to meal times—a last-minute trip to MacDonald's for dinner was now an acceptable alternative—and to life in general. Above all, they preferred planning their day without worrying about someone "yelling" at them, "questioning" their decisions or in some manner reacting negatively to what they chose to do.

Finally, one-fourth of the women (including several mothers who had not originally wanted the divorce) revealed that they were proud of the personal gains they had made since the divorce, particularly regarding their newly gained sense of independence. Contrary to their prior expectations, many mothers learned that they could succeed quite well on their own. Although they may have found work to be hard at first, they now appreciated this opportunity to be "out in the world" and were glad for the external boost to their self-esteem which it provided. Moreover, they enjoyed this chance to meet new people. The women had varied in their degree of dependence on their husbands and the scope of their lives prior to the divorce process. Different achievements were therefore regarded as big steps and sources of pride. One mother, who explained that her whole life had revolved around her house and the children, was very pleased that she had at least mustered the courage to take the children to a restaurant by herself. It had been hard for her "to look for a job, to have a charge account, to get self-serve gas." She felt that the divorce had helped by forcing her to learn that she could go out on her own. In contrast, another mother felt "triumphant" when she bought a house by herself because her husband had always been in charge of major decisions.

Whatever their reactions, the mothers yearned to know that their feelings resulted from the stresses of the divorce process and were normal in that situation. They very much wanted to learn of other women's experiences. Although many commented that it would be impossible to be totally prepared for something so intense which had never been experienced before, they believed that it would have been helpful to have more guidance than they received.

Very unprepared. And when I sought help to try and find out more of what was going to happen to me emotionally and to the kids emotionally as we went through it, I kept getting steered into individual-type therapy or in a group therapy and that wasn't what I needed at all. What I needed was a handbook that said okay, this is what's going to happen, a little Dr. Spock book that says okay you are going to, two days before the divorce is final, feel crummy. You may feel depressed, you may feel angry, you may feel anything at that point but that's going to be a rough time for you. That you may have to deal with what you want to do sexually, what you have to do living wise. But to really describe the emotional side and maybe in terms of the divorce itself. A wide range of things. Not a definite you are going to feel this. But these types of things may happen to you and this is the way, there may be these kinds of feelings that your kids have and all those feelings are normal. . . . So kind of understanding it, to me it's like getting prepared in your household for a fire and how you would get out. That if you know how to get out, then if a fire occurs yes, you're going to panic. Yes, you're going to be worried but you know you have a plan. And what I found was going through the divorce without any plan, and I couldn't find anybody that would help me with it. I didn't know very many divorced people and the people I knew that were divorced were very angry at their spouse and I wasn't interested in being that angry, so I had no model to go through the divorce and not end up with tremendous hatred and tremendous anger and I really could have used something like that.

4

The Mothers' Responses—
The Children's View

All of the interviewed children had formulated views of their mother's reaction to the divorce.[1] The complexity of their descriptions however, ranged from a simple statement that the mother felt "bad" to a detailed explanation of the difficulties of single parenthood. While the children in general demonstrated limited cognitive understanding of the dynamics of their mother's reactions even when they were clearly aware of her upset following the separation, the superficial nature of many responses seemed due in large part to strong defensive barriers against exploring a mother's feelings. The plethora of "I don't knows" and the seeming unwillingness of certain children to try and provide a more in-depth view than was initially volunteered suggests that considerable anxiety and conflicts were connected with examining their mother's divorce experience (e.g., angry wishes that the mother suffer combined with a fear of her consequent unavailability). This was particularly apparent when the child was asked to discuss reactions which would make the mother appear out of control or vulnerable such as depression and fear. The employment of displacement in the interview questions did not seem to mitigate the use of defenses when the child was required to focus on the mother. Commonly, the children's egocentric approach to the divorce also restricted their observations to reactions which directly impinged on their well being (e.g., their mother's moodiness) as well as affecting their interpretation of the behaviors they witnessed (e.g., the mothers were often seen as becoming less patient but the pressures which led to this change were not noted in the majority of cases).

The method by which a child arrived at his conclusions also varied. The child's ability to relate the mother's feelings depended on the mother's manner of handling the divorce situation. It was clear in some children's interviews that their mother had been quite explicit in communicating her reactions. The children were informed of the reasons for the marital breakup (as seen by one or both parents) and the mother's feelings about it. The children's comments in these cases often matched the mother's statements very closely. Other children knew little of the intimate details of the divorce and reflected this ignorance in their more subjective understanding of the mother's behavior. Some seemed satisfied with their lack of knowledge; others were bothered by the mother's failure truly to explain the need for a divorce.

Additionally, the intensity of the mother's reactions to the divorce affected her children's descriptions. In situations where the mother was extremely depressed and/or extremely angry, her upset was so obvious that the children had no difficulty observing it. When the mother's feelings were more subtle or hidden, the children's degree of perceptiveness and ability to empathize came more into play. Over half of the children were able at times to take the jump from noting that their mother was cranky to realizing that she was sad, or from seeing that she was sitting by herself and reading more, to the understanding that she was lonely. The reports of the others were based solely on the concrete behavior, that is, the mother was simply cranky or liked reading. Age (and the corresponding cognitive ability for abstract thinking) was a definite factor here but several of the younger children in the sample appeared more perceptive (perhaps due to lesser defenses) than many of the older children.

Age seemed to be the major factor determining the extent to which the child's projections of his own reactions affected his responses concerning his mother's feelings. The ability to separate one's feelings about an event from another person's feelings seems to develop around the lower end of the age range of this sample. Thus the seven-year-olds, when requested to talk about their mother's reactions to the divorce process, frequently presented a report wherein their own feelings were jumbled with those truly belonging to the parent. For example, one child (aged seven years, two months) started out by saying that his mother felt good about the divorce and then proceeded to state that she worried about his dad's safety and would find it nice if she and his father remarried (which in fact were his own feelings and vastly different from those described by his mother). This sort of projection was rare in children over the age of eight.

Depression

> *Well this is what my mom did. She just cried and cried. And you just get used to it but the first few nights it's like your mother is really sensitive and all this crying might keep you awake at night and you might not get very much sleep.*

Of the 66 children interviewed (52 from families in which both children fell in the sample age range, 14 from families in which only one child was in the targeted sample), 52 indicated that their mother found the divorce process a painfully difficult time. This accounts for 36 mothers and thus almost duplicates the statistics on the mothers' self-report, although in seven cases only one of the two children interviewed described this reaction.

Usually the children's descriptions emphasized their observation that mothers are saddened and/or hurt by a separation. Their conclusions were most commonly based on the fact that they had seen their mother cry. Many were unaccustomed to seeing their mother upset and gave a great deal of significance to the few incidents they witnessed. Others reported frequent crying for a period of up to a year: at night when the children were supposedly asleep, at the dinner table when the absence of the father was particularly obvious or whenever the issue of divorce was raised. The cause of the mother's upset was rarely elaborated in any detail. Usually the children stated that their mother was sad because she missed their father, missed the good times she had in her marriage, or simply "because of the divorce." However, when the father initiated the divorce, particularly when he went on to a new relationship, the children's explanations were often more involved. They discussed their mother's confusion about the divorce, her continued positive feelings for her husband, and her hurt that he left her.

She might cry thinking about his dad getting another wife. . . . My mom cried a lot because she still liked my dad a little when my dad got married. And grandma wrote the family and told my mom what she looked like and she looked just like my mom almost and my mom really cried.

While recognizing that the divorce process was at times a painful experience for their mother, 10 children explained that her reaction was a mixture of sadness and happiness. They stated that she was sad because she was lonely or because it was difficult to adjust to being on her own after years of marriage but that she was also glad to be separated. An additional 15 children described their mother as sad when the decision to divorce was first made but considered this reaction to be very short-lived. In part, the children's depiction of a quick recovery was due to their reliance on concrete evidence for their conclusions. Thus, while not observing any particular reaction to the contrary, they assumed that their mother was no longer sad because they no longer saw her cry. Some children explained that their mother wanted the divorce and was relieved and/or happy once it was underway. A couple of children attributed her new happiness to involvement with a new man.

Only in rare instances was the scope of their mother's depression recognized. In describing their mother's sadness, the children at times hinted at a clinical picture of depression, such as when they discussed her failure to attend to normal daily responsibilities or the ease with which she became overwhelmed by trivial mishaps, but the issue was not addressed explicitly. Thirteen children commented that their mother appeared "in her own world," "wrapped up in herself," or "preoccupied" but, unlike the mothers, only two children attributed this reaction to an underlying problem. Just five children picked up on the importance of their mother's lack of energy. The mother's low self-esteem during the divorce process, as exemplified by assertions that she felt worthless and unlovable, was also seldom described by the children. In the few cases when this reaction was noted, the children were mainly aware of their mother's self-doubts because she had repeatedly expressed them to the children, not because they demonstrated unusual insight into their mother's difficulties. For example, one child commented that her mother had often said to her, "Why does this have to happen to me. Why can't I have a husband that loves me and will stay with me?"

Loneliness

> [*She feels lonely*] *sometimes because, she has her kids to talk to but she can't talk in a grown-up way. She can't talk about grown-up things like she used to talk with her husband. There's no one to tell and it's like the whole world has deserted you.*

The children's descriptions of their mother's loneliness were remarkably similar to the mothers' own descriptions. As was true in the interviews with the women, a small number of children contended that their mother was lonely primarily when they were away. The weekends when they visited their father were seen as the loneliest times. Most of the children who were able to elaborate reasons for their belief that their mother was lonely, recognized that she missed adult male companionship. Like the child quoted above, they sensed their inability to fill the gap created when their father left home. To a small extent the children confused general loneliness with missing the ex-husband but usually they were able to differentiate between wanting someone nearby from wanting a particular person. Their discussion of this issue revealed that the mother missed having another adult around with whom to discuss things, to help her when she found a task difficult, to sleep with, to give her affection, and just to be available when she was home.

 Loneliness was discussed by more of the interviewed children than any other reaction their mother experienced with the exception of anger (i.e., 56 children: 14 spontaneously, 42 in response to a direct question). Although the children did not frequently address this reaction without some prompting from the interviewer—it was common for children only to mention such emotions as sad and happy, and issues relating to them, before direct questioning—they readily agreed that it existed. In the large majority of cases they were able to provide some details about it. Perhaps because it was a reaction that many shared, they were especially empathic about the mother's feelings in this area. When not specifically told so by their mother, the children based their view that she was lonely on her tendency to sit by herself "not doing anything," "drag around," "mope around," and look "bored." Additionally, a few related that they learned that their mother was lonely by overhearing phone conversations with friends. Often it seemed that they simply placed themselves in their mother's shoes and concluded that she would be lonely.

Sense of Isolation

Well like the friends she used to have, they didn't really believe in divorce and now she's got divorced, she doesn't have these friends anymore but she liked them.

Only 5 children reported that their mothers felt isolated from their former social network. The common contention of the women in this study that married friends pull away when a divorce takes place was expressed by only the above-quoted child.

Many children however, revealed that they recognized this reaction in their discussions of how the mother might feel better after the divorce or in their descriptions of with whom she socializes now. Twelve children observed that meeting a new man and dating in general cheered their mother immensely. Six children indicated that their mother socialized with different friends now than before the divorce. Singles' groups such as Parents Without Partners and work were mentioned as places for meeting new people. Finally, eight children considered getting married again to be a remedy for all of their mother's problems following the separation. Some of these children had reached this conclusion because they had witnessed the very positive effect of their mother's new marriage but the others presented it as a solution without any real man in mind.

Anger

She's been very angry at him. . . . She would get mean at him and start a fight and stuff and have him, give him a really dirty face. . . . [Both parents] act meaner than they used to. . . . Well just because, like sometimes they would do things for each other and now they don't ever do a thing for each other.

Unlike the mothers, the children were quite open and direct in discussing the anger they observed on the part of their parents. Sixty out of the 66 children in the sample mentioned that their mother had been angry at their father at some point since the divorce process began. Thirty-six children commented on this reaction to the divorce without any inquiry from the interviewer. The others readily admitted when questioned that anger had been evident. Besides the obvious anger displayed in verbal (or in a few cases, physical) battles between the parents, the children discussed the hostility apparent in the mother's "put-downs" of the father, her use of "naughty words" in referring to him, her quick temper when the children talked about him, her facial expressions during a phone conversation with him, and the way she sometimes went "around shoving things" after she spoke to him. Most often, the children interpreted their mother's anger as an expected and unavoidable aspect of divorce. About one-half of the children viewed the father as provoking her hostile behavior but only rarely did this perception result in the children sharing their mother's overall negative opinion of her ex-husband.

The children's explanations of their mother's anger focused on all steps of the divorce process. Fights toward the end of the marriage, as well as the "yelling and screaming" which occurred while the legal proceedings were underway, were described. Some children, like the girl quoted at the outset of this section, revealed that their parents' animosity was still apparent, or in fact, appeared to have escalated as time elapsed. For example, one twelve-year-old stated that her parents "hate each other now"; several children related that their mother currently refuses to see their father. In addition to the continuance of anger connected to events which caused the marital breakup, the mother's present hostility was commonly attributed to the burden of all her responsibilities and to problems connected to child support payments (e.g., late payment, the father attempting to reduce payment, etc.).

A major source of anger during each phase of the divorce process, according to the children, was the father's involvement with a new woman. In the view of the children, divorced women find it very difficult to deal with the remarriage of their husband and the subsequent establishment of a relationship between the children and their stepmother. Moreover, the children explained that the adjustment to the knowledge of the father's new wife is made even more hurtful when the husband lies about his interest in another woman and her role in the intiation of the divorce. One eleven-year-old illustrated this point in her response to a question about whether her mother was ever angry at her father:

> *Yeah, because he would still come back here and when she found out that, like she drove by and, she found out where the girl was living, and she drove by and she saw him and her together and then she didn't like that very much but she didn't tell him. But when he came back she said "why didn't you tell me?" She would have liked it better if he would have told her he was going out instead of lying all the time.*

Twelve fathers from the families studied in this research had remarried by the time of the interview. The children in seven of these families made a point of saying that this event angered their mother.

Whereas the mothers often expressed their anger at their ex-husband through issues which derived from concern about the children, the children viewed the situation differently. Other than anger related to inadequate child support payments, criticism of the father's actions involving the children was not mentioned as a cause of their mother's antagonistic feelings. The children did however, feel that more anger was directed at them now than before the divorce. Five children concluded that they were receiving anger which was really meant for their father. The others just knew that their mother yelled at them whenever she was in a bad mood which was stated to be a frequent occurrence. Her mood swings were typically found to be unpredictable and confusing.

> *Just every day she'd change her actions, you know. One day she'd be really screaming mad and another day she'd be really pleasant and everything so I don't know how she really felt.*

Twenty-five children in all, described a change in their mother's behavior towards them which involved her becoming "less nice," less patient, or "short-fused." Thirty-eight children commented that their mother had become moody.

Guilt

> *She was never guilty for getting divorced but she probably feels guilty because we really loved our dad and she didn't have to get divorced.*

The issue of guilt was rarely addressed by the children before they were asked a leading question. While not using the exact word, four children spontaneously communicated their recognition that their mother had experienced guilt related to the divorce. Twenty-one children responded positively to the interviewer's inquiry about whether their mother felt guilty but even then, 10 of these children failed to elaborate on their response in any way. It seems likely that the majority of children do not perceive their mother as feeling guilty nor do they think to report this on their own because this is a reaction which except in unusual circumstances is not readily visible. A considerable capacity for empathy is thus required on the part of the child. It is also possible that the concept of guilt is not yet well understood by the age group of this sample although the children who described this reaction displayed no confusion about its meaning.

Additionally, it is conceivable that the number, noted above, of children who were considered to have observed their mother feeling guilty, is an inflated one. The children's attribution of guilt to the mother may actually, in many cases, be a reflection of their own anger at the mother for separating from their father and not an accurate statement of how they viewed her response to the divorce process.

In two-thirds of those cases where the child stated a source for the mother's guilt, the negative impact of the divorce on the children was seen as her primary concern. The mothers were believed to feel guilty for "not having her children brought up with a father" and, more generally, for voluntarily making a decision to which the children objected. The other aspects of the divorce experience noted by the mothers to create guilt feelings such as their dating, their work, or their self-improvement, were not mentioned by the children in this context.

Fear

A mother would worry about getting a job and getting enough money to feed the kids and herself and trying to get along in the winter and not getting stuck.

Whether because children are unable to conceive of their parents as being frightened (due to intellectual limitations and defenses against recognizing that their parents might feel weak and vulnerable) or because the mothers worked hard to maintain a strong facade, fear was emphasized much less in the child interviews than it was in the interviews with the women. With the exception of concerns related to financial matters, none of the various fears discussed by the mothers were referred to by more than one-third of the children.

Eleven children, one-sixth of the sample, from 11 different families observed that their mother had been much more "nervous" than usual following the separation. Several were aware of the many practical decisions involved in a divorce settlement, explaining that their mother worried about who was going to keep the house or how she would find another, the custody issue, and the legal process itself. The mothers' nervousness was also attributed to their concern as to how they would succeed at taking care of their kids without a husband and managing a job. More generally, the children talked of their mother's fear of the future and her tendency to "worry a lot more about everything" because the situation was so new to her.

The children were relatively well informed of the family's financial situation. Although half of the 52 children who agreed that money matters were a cause for concern provided only an unelaborated "yes" to a question as to whether this reaction existed, the remaining youngsters presented it early on in their interview as an important aspect of the divorce experience. Perhaps reflecting their own fears that the continuity of their lives would be further disrupted by needing to move, being unable to afford certain items to which they were accustomed or that basic necessities would become unaffordable, the children commonly focused on their mother's fear she would be unable to support her children. They often then listed the many costs involved in taking care of a family and maintaining a home such as food, clothes, furniture, electricity, the car, and house payments. Several children stated that their mother had been afraid she would have difficulty finding a job. They frequently knew of the mother's reliance on their father's child-support payments and were aware of whether he paid regularly or was lax about this responsibility. For example, one eight and one-half-year-old explained:

> *Well, she's having a little trouble finding a job and she usually doesn't make much money. See I don't think she could really live if my dad didn't have to pay child support 'cause she only gets like a hundred dollars a week and that's not very much to support both of us and pay for food and all that stuff and clothes.*

Twenty-two children, including seven sibling pairs, believed that their mother had been worried about them during the divorce process. Given that this concern was not asked about directly by the interviewer, it is likely that more children would have indicated this to be the case if the issue had been raised. Like the mothers themselves reported, the children noted that their mother worried about their reactions to the divorce, fearing that they would have difficulty accepting it and adjusting to their new circumstances. A number of children observed that their mother delayed telling them about the upcoming divorce because of this fear, and worried that the children would not understand why it was necessary. For the most part, the children believed that their mother's concern was based on a wish to avoid causing them any pain. They indicated that their mother was sad whenever they felt badly because of the separation. Four children additionally specified that their mother worried that they would blame her for getting the divorce and be angry as a result.

The Pressures of Single Parenthood

> *She'll have to, see like my mom never worked 'cause she doesn't like the idea of having to go to work and coming home and taking care of the house. Like she's two people in one and that's really hard.*

The majority of interviewed children did not appear to be aware of the overwhelming nature of the demands placed on a single parent. The 27 children who addressed some aspect of this issue however, seemed especially understanding of the pressures with which their mother was dealing.

Ten children focused on the difficulty of caring for them without a husband. Many labeled this responsibility the hardest thing about a divorce. While not always stating so explicitly, the children clearly recognized the problems caused because the mother had no one to assist her "especially when they are acting difficult," no relief unless they were with their dad, and no one to share in the decision making involved in child raising.

Attending to their daily care was discussed by several children as only one task among a long list which their mother must accomplish. Twenty children expressed their awareness of the extent to which their mother's responsibilities increased following the separation. They talked about how hard it was for her to work full time and then still need to take care of the kids and the house when she returned home. Her emotional and physical fatigue at the end of the day, particularly in those instances where the woman was newly adjusting to full-time employment, was obvious. This exhaustion was concretized by many children in their description of the one responsibility which in their view overloaded their mother.

> *Well, if she works and she comes home and her children are hungry when she gets home, she'll have to cook dinner right away. She don't like that either.*

The mothers' lack of patience since the divorce, discussed earlier, is relevant here as well and is probably the children's version of what the women described as their reduced capacity for parenting. (The women however, were rarely as detailed as the children in describing the ways in which parenting was affected.)

The pressures created by the need to adopt, at least in part, the father's role in the family, were also recognized by many of the children. In numerous cases, they perceived their mother's role prior to the divorce as that of a traditional housewife/mother. The assumption of the chores formerly relegated to the father, in addition to the necessity of working outside the home, was considered to be a major factor affecting her sense of being overwhelmed. Some children cited particular tasks which the mother found burdensome such as fixing the cars, paying the bills, making household repairs, or doing yardwork. For example, the same child quoted at the beginning of this section went on to say:

She'll have to do more stuff. Like if she's not used to going outside in the cold and working in the yard. That's sort of hard because some moms like to stay in the house and be really neat and nice and warm so that's hard.

In the process of describing the pressures of single parenthood, the women had also discussed the difficulty of coping with some of the children's reactions to the divorce. The children certainly observed their mother's annoyance when they brought up the topic of the divorce or were "fussy" but did not appear to notice that specific reactions on their part were especially troublesome for their mother.

Positive Reactions

But I think you know, she told us it was a good decision to make. It was better for their lives and everybody else's.

Although most of the children recognized that the divorce process evoked many negative feelings for their mother, on the whole they considered it to be a more positive experience for her than she herself described. This discrepancy between the reports of the children and the mothers may be explained in several ways. First, it is evident from the children's interviews that children with their tendency to see things as black and white, commonly assumed that their mother was happy following the divorce because they could not understand why else she would separate from their father. For example, one ten-year-old boy followed his assertion that his mother was happy after the divorce occurred by elaborating:

Like if she didn't like him, then she liked another man, it's better for her to break up with him if she didn't like him.

Additionally, the mothers' sense of a progression in feelings over time was more clear than the children's. Thus, while the women did not typically look back on the period following the divorce as a happy one, they reported that their gradual adjustment to their new status and the freedom from the tension inherent in the breakdown of a marriage have allowed for increasingly more happy moments. The children's view of the mother's positive demeanor now seemed to shadow in some cases, their memories of her reactions at the time of the divorce. The children also blurred the difference between happiness as a reaction to the divorce and happiness as a response to good things in general (i.e., happiness because of the divorce versus happiness in spite of the divorce).

Unless they were exceedingly depressed, the women certainly had cheerful periods during the divorce process but this does not mean that they were basically happy. Finally, the children's lesser emphasis on their mother's negative feelings may have served defensive purposes. Recognition of the depth or duration of their mother's pain may have been too full of anxiety to be incorporated into the children's view of her reactions.

Thirty-four children, including seven sibling pairs, spontaneously related that their mother experienced relief at some point during the divorce process. Fourteen children discussed their mother's relief when the decision to divorce was first made; 20 children noted her relief when the actual divorce was granted. The first group of children explained that their mother felt better now that she had taken steps to remedy a bad situation.

Like I knew she was really glad that she finally decided to get a divorce because she'd been thinking about that for a long, long time.

They stated that she was glad that she no longer needed to interact with her husband on a daily basis. The latter group indicated that their mother felt relieved to know it was "all over" and that she and the children could get on with their lives. Above all, both groups emphasized the importance of the cessation of fighting. Many children recalled the period preceding the separation or when the court proceedings were underway as a time of constant arguing. The absence of someone yelling at her was thus seen to be the major improvement in the mother's situation.

Twenty-seven children, referring to 18 mothers, reported that their mother felt happy when the separation and/or the divorce took place. This view was frequently supported by statements that their mother had wanted the divorce and that she believed the current arrangement was better for everyone. Although some children talked about their mother's feelings as a mixture of "good and bad" (as indicated earlier when the issue of depression was addressed), many thought that she adjusted rapidly to the divorce and felt largely positive about it. Several children described her as now being generally more relaxed than during the marriage.

5

The Children's Responses

The previous two chapters focused on the mothers' reactions to the divorce process, first as understood by themselves and then as viewed by their children. In order to conclude the discussion of the individual family member's divorce experience, the next two chapters will examine the children's responses to their parents' separation and divorce.

In observing the children's approach to discussing themselves during the interview, several distinct styles were apparent. As was the case with the mothers, the children's feelings appeared to range from acceptance of the divorce as something past to current involvement with all the feelings it evoked. Unlike the mothers however, there were several instances in which a discrepancy existed between the content of the interview and the child's overall manner of presentation. Thus, there was a group of children who openly described themselves as still very upset about the divorce while remaining quite composed and another group who stated that they had accepted the divorce but clearly found discussing it to be very upsetting. A few others appeared calm and removed from the issues addressed but maintained this stance by "forgetting" much of the divorce experience. On the other hand, there were many children who related their reactions to the divorce in vivid detail but seemed relatively content with their new family structure and lifestyle.

Despite the existence of the common latency-age defenses evident in the above descriptions, the children on the whole provided a more complete picture of their feelings about their parents' divorce than was expected. Although the use of displacement in the interview schedule was shown to have only limited impact on the children's report of mothers' reactions, the phrasing of the questions combined with the interviewer's appeal for the children's help in preparing others in a similar situation seemed successful in eliciting a great deal of information about the children's own experience.

While some children, in reporting their reactions, addressed the many different aspects of the divorce experience, it was not uncommon for a child to focus almost solely on one facet. Most frequently, the central event for these children was the departure of the father from the home. Whenever it made logical sense, they answered a question in terms of this issue. Therefore, the "hardest thing" was not seeing their dad; they "worried" about when they would see him. Another change which elicited this type of response was the rift between the parents.

As stated earlier, most of the questions in the section of the interview dealing with the children's view of their own reactions were asked using displacement. However, as will be seen in the examples provided in this chapter, the children varied in the form of their reply. Some children consistently continued the use of displacement, discussing the issues in terms of the feelings of another child. Other children at times answered by referring specifically to their own reactions. Since it is believed that all the children's responses are based on their own experience, to prevent confusion the findings are generally reported as if the children always were speaking about themselves.

Surprise and Trouble Believing It Was Happening

When they tell him that, just when they tell him, he's surprised that they're getting divorced because they did so well. He thought that they did so well and they didn't think so—that's what makes him surprised when they tell you.

Regardless of the reasons for the marital breakdown or the manner in which the parents' problems were manifested, the children are unprepared for the divorce. Sixty out of the 66 children interviewed stated that they had been surprised by the news of the divorce and/or couldn't believe that it was actually taking place. In the eyes of most of the children, the parental separation occurred "suddenly" with no forewarning. No connection with previous events was made.

Well he would be surprised because all of a sudden, they just told him.

Well I'd come home and they were packing up and leaving, and you wouldn't know what to do.

The children's shocked reaction to the plans for divorce derived from their typical view of the predivorce marital relationship as a positive one. Chronic problems were apparently not noticed or successfully denied. Additionally, fights which at present loomed very large in the children's memory were at the time considered relatively unimportant. In general, the children simply assumed that their parents were happy with each other.

Well I thought they were happily married, you know. They never used to fight.

Yes [I was surprised]. I didn't know they were having trouble. I thought they were getting along really good but unfortunately, they weren't.

Efforts at denial were so strong that once the parents had filed for divorce, there was often a lack of acknowledgment of the inevitability of the final papers. The children reportedly dealt with the situation by convincing themselves that the separation was temporary.

I knew he was moving out and I knew they weren't getting along too well, but I didn't think they'd get a divorce.

Like saying that your dad just went out for a couple of minutes. Just keep saying to yourself that he'll be coming back, that in a couple of days he'll come home.

Each step taken by the parents towards the actual divorce was therefore another surprise.

Confusion

[I wanted to know] why did you get divorced, really, and she answered that one but I don't get why we can't all live together and she hasn't answered it.

In keeping with their lack of preparation for the divorce, the children frequently found the chain of events quite confusing. Although the interviewer had not anticipated the prevalence of this response and thus had not asked about it directly, over half of the sample (i.e., 37 out of 66 children) referred to it in some manner. Most frequently, the children's difficulty in understanding this upheaval in their family resulted from their failure to see any reason for the divorce. The simple explanations provided by their parents were inadequate to alleviate their concerns. The children longed to know more about why the separation was necessary.

... and then she feels mad because her mom tells her that she's going to get divorced but doesn't tell her why or how or when.

Moreover, aspects of certain explanations such as assurances by the mother that she continued to love her husband, added to their confusion. Although children were quick to provide "the family line" when first asked about the cause for the divorce, they often indicated later that they still had unanswered questions. These questions addressed basic issues including "why they didn't get along," and "why couldn't they work it out." Despite the common assertion of the mothers that they made a point of telling the children that they had nothing to do with the parents' problems, 14 children (21 percent of the sample) mentioned that they feared that they were "kind of the cause of everything." Failing to understand an alternative explanation, they overestimated their own power and figured that in some manner their bad behavior had pushed their father away.

> *We thought he left us. I thought it was because I wasn't doing good in school or wasn't acting right or something.*

> *I always asked for things and I was a nag.*

> *I've acted up all my life.*

Approximately a quarter of the children who indicated that they were confused, had trouble comprehending the actual actions of their parents. A few children revealed that they did not understand what the word "divorce" meant and therefore did not know what to expect. For example, one child said he was confused when his dad left home, explaining that he "thought he was still going to live there even though they were divorced." The others were not cognizant of the fact that divorce procedures were underway because their mothers reportedly never directly told them what was happening. One child, who eventually learned of the divorce from overhearing her mother talking to her friends, related:

> *When my dad moved out it was like a couple of months after he left and we would feel like "oh, where is dad? Isn't he coming home for dinner or anything like that?" It was just like that for a couple of months.*

Other children knew they were moving but did not know why their father was not coming with them.

Sadness

> *I felt pretty sad 'cause you know, you live with somebody that long and just real quick he goes away. It just makes you feel bad.*

As was true for the mothers in talking about themselves, the children's descriptions of their reactions to the divorce process emphasized the intense sadness they had experienced. There was universal agreement that divorce is an upsetting affair. The children did not want the divorce to occur and typically could think of little or nothing which improved in their lives because of it. Each step of the divorce—the decision, the father leaving home, the final decree—caused new pain.

> *Well it's a sort of sad feeling. And you really don't want them to get divorced when you hear about it.*

> *I didn't feel too good because I didn't want my dad to leave.*

> *It would be like, it would be sad, and like if they got a final decree and she'd know that and her parents might have told her and she would feel even worse maybe.*

> *Well it's just like every answer that I've been telling you. I didn't want them to get a divorce and everything like a normal kid would just say.*

Children whose father failed to keep in regular contact with them commonly cited a particular source of their distress: they believed that their father no longer cared for them. A similar feeling was expressed by children of men who were now living with a new family. The children perceived that their father had replaced the affection he had for them with loving feelings for his stepchildren.

While a few children stated that they felt sad for just a brief period, the majority indicated they remained dejected for six months to over a year. (Although the children's ability to report a time span accurately is certainly doubtful in many cases, their desire to show that the sadness lasted for a long time is clear.)

> *Well I think you should tell her that it will probably hurt for a long time too. About a half a year and then she'll sort of all get over it but sometimes it would come back and hurt a little more but that would be later on.*

Many children still found the thought of the divorce to be painful.

> *I still can't get over it . . . that my dad keeps coming and going and coming and going. . . . [A girl would feel] really sad because when she starts thinking about it, if you get a sore and you keep thinking about it, it won't go away.*

It was evident in examining the children's responses to the interview that their sadness occurred in two phases: an acute phase which accompanied their disbelief, described previously, and a less intense but long-lasting phase which followed an acceptance of the divorce as an unalterable fact. The more articulate children communicated this directly. For example, one twelve-year-old boy who reported that he felt numb when he was first told of the upcoming divorce and very sad when his dad moved out, went on to explain:

> *Well you'll always feel sad a little, but in some way or another, but it just, you learn to live with it, you know, keep going.*

A nine-year-old girl remarked similarly:

> *Well when it very first happened, I was sort of upset. . . . I was crying and just felt very bad. . . . Then she'll probably start getting used to the idea and think that they're getting a divorce and she can't do anything about it.*

She later continues:

> *For me, the most hardest thing for me was getting used to the idea that they were going to get a divorce and then after it happened to get a little more used to it.*

Events which remind the children of the divorce and underline the difference between them and children in two-parent families cause the pain to resurface.

> *My friend would always be going places with her dad and stuff. It would make me feel kind of weird. Well like see, like in school we have to, they always say parents and that brings it up again.*

Depression

> C: *I didn't tell very many of my friends. They just found out.*
> I: How come you didn't tell them?
> C: *Well I don't want like the whole world to know that they're divorced.*
> I: How did you feel when your friends asked you about your dad not being there?
> C: *Well, I sort of thought about it. What I should tell them. I didn't want to lie and I didn't want to tell them they were divorced. I didn't have a choice.*
> I: And how did you feel when they knew?
> C: *I just, guessed they, I guess they just made me feel good 'cause I asked them if they'd tell anybody and they said no.*

Aspects of depression as a clinical syndrome emerge during the interviews but are clearly not labeled as such by the children. An inability to cope with daily demands stemming from a loss of the ego's control over stress, which played a central role in the mothers' reports, was given relatively little attention in the child interviews. In referring to the intense pain they experienced at the time of the separation the children did describe being preoccupied with thoughts of the divorce and profoundly sad but they did not generally present themselves as overwhelmed by their feelings once the sense of crisis had subsided. At least in their memories, they were soon able to compartmentalize their reaction to the divorce and resume normal activity. A small minority of children discussed an overall lethargy, a withdrawal from people and difficulty concentrating in school.

Well I was sort of upset you know, like down in the dumps and it was hard to do my school work.

Predominant in the children's self-report were indications of a sharp lowering of self-esteem. This was chiefly reflected in the children's explanations of their discomfort relating to peers. Unaffected by the increasing statistics of divorcing families, the children were embarrassed by their situation and felt that their parents' separation set them apart from their former friends. Over half of the sample, 37 children, related that they postponed telling anyone about the separation until the truth was unavoidable and felt uncomfortable when doing so. As was the case with the child quoted at the beginning of this section, they told others only when asked and dreaded the word being spread around school.

[When telling my friends I felt] well sort of secretive I guess. Don't go yapping off your big mouth. . . . I guess you just don't want the whole school to know that your parents are divorced or separated or something. It's sort of private.

Most frequently the children described their discomfort as feeling "different" from everyone else. The divorce had somehow made them less worthy than other children so that interactions with children whose parents were not divorced became strained. Additionally, many equated the divorce with no longer having a father, a difference which itself embarrassed them.

I figured they'd go "ooh, you don't have a dad, that's too bad."

Well it started out that I was a little bit scared to tell anybody because all my friends have two parents and then I only had one, and I'd feel sort of weird.

It appears that the children's sense of self was still largely dependent on the family structure which their parents had provided prior to the separation. The divorce thus not only caused the breakup of their family but also threatened the foundation of their self-esteem.

Missing Dad

Yeah, miss him for a year or something or maybe the rest of his life.

Unlike the mothers, the children always linked their postseparation distress, at least in part, to the loss of their father. They reacted strongly to this loss when it first occurred and continued to do so. Sixty-four out of 66 children stated that they missed their father. Fifty-one of these children (77 percent of the total group) referred to this reaction before it was mentioned by the interviewer, often before they addressed any other aspect of the divorce.

While, according to the children, proximity to the home of their father and frequent contact with him was the crucial factor in their ability to adjust to the divorce, seeing him regularly did not prevent their missing his daily presence at home. They wanted to be at hand when he returned from work, spend each evening with him available to them, and go to sleep knowing he was in a room close by.

Most typically, the children stated that they missed the father himself, not what they did with him. In other words, even if a substitute was available to take the father's place in the family, their "real" father would still be special. In explaining how they missed their father, the children often demonstrated a rather circular form of reasoning. For example, one child first said, in describing what a boy would feel when his parents divorce, that he would miss his dad because he wouldn't "be able to see him very much." When asked what was hardest about a divorce, he replied, "being without a father." His response to the interviewer's question as to what made that hard was "you don't get to see him that much." He continued that the way a boy could make things better was to see his dad.

When the children could elaborate in more detail why they missed their father, an idealized portrayal of the predivorce father-child relationship was commonly communicated. Long lists of shared activities were offered as the children looked back nostalgically on the time when their father lived at home.

. . . miss his father helping him do things and build things and playing football and stuff. Building, sports, and playing games with him. And help him build a new bicycle, and help him build his train set, and help him build his race set. And play with him with his battleship.

Well her dad won't be there anymore. There's some things that she can't do anymore because her dad wasn't there. . . . Well my dad used to always pick me up and give me a piggyback ride upstairs to my bedroom, or pick me up and swing me around or something like that.

Even regular visits were found unsatisfactory in part because they were compared to the child's recollection of extensive periods together on a daily basis. Boys in particular, maintained a strong loyalty to their father which they attributed to their shared male status. They equated the departure of the father due to the parental separation with their losing an ally. For instance, two boys aged twelve-and-one-half and seven years responded to the question "What are the hardest things he'll have to face?" as follows:

> *Not having a dad to talk to man to man and not having a dad to play sports and stuff like that with, not having a dad to fix things, like help you on sports, and not to be there all the time, only seeing him weekends, things like that.*

> *Being the only boy in the house. Like if I want to go someplace and it's someplace that they don't want to go I have to go someplace that they want to because they got more people on their side.*

Overall, the children presented mixed reports about changes in their relationship with their father. Some said that he became nicer and more attentive since the divorce so that they felt closer to him now. Others stated that he seemed uninterested and that they hardly saw him. A small group of girls however (most of whom were aged ten and over) seemed mainly disillusioned with him. They explained that although they missed him at first, this reaction was either no longer experienced or far less intense.

> I: Did you ever miss your dad?
> G: *I did. I don't anymore. I've adjusted to it and I'm beginning more and more to understand what my dad is really like. And he's becoming more and more obnoxious everytime I see him.*

These girls, in fact, reacted (with regard to their feelings toward their father) much as their mother did, closely identifying with her in her hurt and anger. It seems likely that the reemergence of Oedipal wishes as adolescence approaches causes some girls to experience the divorce as if they too were abandoned wives. The separation pushes them to reject their father and cement their identification with their mother. In contrast, preadolescent boys, as a group, conveyed intense yearning for their father and revealed in the difficulty with which they kept their tears suppressed that they found it particularly hard to adjust to living without him.

Missing the Parental Couple or the Predivorce Family

> *When they got divorced, you know they're all together and then they got divorced and you feel sort of sad because you don't get to see your dad*

and mom at the same time. They would want to see their father a lot and their mother a lot and they wouldn't get to see them at the same time.

Twenty children (30.3 percent of those interviewed) explained that missing their father was only one part of a larger picture. Visiting their father temporarily solved one of their problems but also created another. Since they could no longer interact with both parents together, the children were faced with a situation wherein they must always miss one parent or the other. Even when visits with their father proceeded smoothly they thus were still not completely satisfied because their mother was not present.

[A boy would feel] worried that they wouldn't see him anymore. Well they would see him but they'd see their dad at different times and their mom at different times. And so when you're at the dad's you'd sort of miss your mom and when you're at your mom's you'd sort of miss your dad.

Like he might want always to see whoever moved and when he gets over there he might always want to see the person that's here. He wants to see both of them at the same time.

In the same vein, several children discussed how much they missed the family togetherness. Although they may now go on outings with their father or mother separately, these activities somehow do not seem as enjoyable as what they remembered before the divorce.

It's just that they wouldn't see their family anymore all together and doing things together like going to an amusement park or something. They wouldn't be doing that together. . . . And that wouldn't make me feel together.

While this reaction to the divorce was only discussed by slightly less than one third of the sample, the numbers seem large indeed when it is considered that the interviewer failed to mention it in any way. Children who responded to much of the interview with one-word answers or "I don't knows" were very articulate in describing this feeling, which underlines its importance to them.

Loneliness

There's certain things that you do with your dad that you can't do with your mom cause she won't want to play catch or nothing or go see scary movies or nothing and after awhile you must sit and sit and be bored and your mom is having fun and she's playing cards with all her friends and you get really lonely.

When the women talked about loneliness, they discussed the difficulty of being without a husband. In parallel fashion, 17 children (25.8 percent of the sample) stated that they felt lonely because they did not have a father living with them. However, 35 children (53 percent) felt that they were in part losing the attentions of both their father and their mother. Seven other children (10.6 percent) agreed when questioned that they had experienced loneliness but failed to elaborate this reaction in any way.

The children who focused solely on the loneliness stemming from the absence of their father often talked about this reaction in conjunction with discussing how much they missed him. In fact, several children simply stated that they were lonely because their father moved out or because they missed him. Unlike the mothers therefore, the children's loneliness (as they understood it) resulted from the loss of a specific person. They both wished he were present and felt lonely because a gap was created in their lives by his leaving.

Yes I felt lonely. Because when my dad left, it took a couple days after, we usually had this little chair that was always my dad's chair and everytime I looked over there, there wasn't anyone in it and I felt, I wished that someone was sitting there just like my dad.

A boy would feel lonely because he doesn't have any daddy anymore.

Well just missing whoever moves away, just missing them a lot and it's like having nobody around and you want to see your parent really bad.

The children explained that they found it difficult to adjust to living with just one parent because their house felt empty to them. Children who had little contact with their father emphasized the connection between infrequent visitation and their loneliness.

If they get divorced from their dad, they'd be lonely because they hadn't seen their dad for a long time.

When loneliness was discussed in terms of a change in the relationship with both parents, the children primarily talked about the time they now spent alone. In addition to losing out on the time formerly spent with their father, the present circumstances of their mother's life caused her to be less available. Most frequently, the children discussed how hard it was for them to have their mother working full time. Many women's job schedules were such that they were home for very few of the children's waking hours.

Mom was working more often and we didn't get to see her, or my dad wouldn't come over for months or for weeks or anything. And it was really lonely because she would get home about 9:30 p.m. and it was school time so I usually go to bed at about 10:00 p.m. so I really didn't see much of her.

Yes, sometimes I'd feel really neglected or like I didn't even have a mother or a father because my mom would always be working and I would only be able to see my dad on the weekends.

You'd feel pretty lonely because your mom always has to work or your dad because there's no one else to get money unless you work all day, then you don't have them with you most of the time.

Children who were accustomed to being greeted by their mother when they returned home from school felt especially bad to have this routine ended.

The mothers' lives as divorced women also typically involved dating or socializing more regularly with female friends. The children therefore frequently commented that they missed being with their mother when she was out at night. While she may have spent some time alone with friends prior to the divorce, each incident was noticed more by the children now since their father was not home to take care of them in her absence.

[Mom] goes out more . . . into a bar or somewhere or a friend's house. [When mom goes out more, a kid would feel] not really happy. 'Cause she'd be, she doesn't really spend hardly any of her time with the children.

Mom goes out more. . . . She's always going to dinner or out to lunch and she just went to Chicago for the weekend. . . . It would make them feel lonely inside.

Even when their mother was home, she still was not seen to be as free to devote her time to the children. The children stated that they were lonely when the mother's many responsibilities kept her continually busy. Furthermore, they related that it was hard with only one parent because when she was occupied, there was no one else available to play.

Well like see, we used to play games and stuff while mom was doing the dishes or something and now mom doesn't have time to play games or anything like that.

Yes [a girl would feel lonely] because if your parents get a divorce, then you can't, the parent that you're living with will have to have more responsibilities and you can't do as much as if two people were doing it.

Finally, in talking about why they felt lonely, a few children concentrated on the psychological changes in their parents following the divorce. The father's seeming lack of interest in maintaining close contact with the children combined with the self-absorption of the mother (stemming from her depression and her attempts to cope with the divorce herself) made the children feel basically abandoned.

It's like you're losing your parents and you're left alone . . . like you don't got the same parents.

She should expect that her mom would be going out, you know going out with men, that her dad, she can expect her dad to be going out with women and she should feel that nobody loves her and that she should run away. That's how I feel. . . . I feel lonely because I have no one. . . . I don't know, it's just she doesn't talk to me and I don't talk to her. It's just like we are two strangers.

Hope of Reconciliation

It would be a pretty nice dream. My dad has a girlfriend and he didn't like her so he came back to my mom. . . . I don't like him being remarried. I think he should marry my mom.

Given that the children were clear in communicating that they did not want the divorce in the first place and that they longed for their father's return, it is understandable that they dreamt about their parents reconciling. Fifty-six children (almost 85 percent of the sample) claimed to have experienced this reaction. More than 13 percent of the children considered this to be the only way to "make things better" following a divorce. The mother's insistence that a reconciliation would never take place or the child's realization that the happy fantasy he just had was not reality brought on new pain.

. . . and then you go ask them and they say "no we're never going to get back together" and the feelings are shattered.

I feel sort of sad when I wake up and realize that it's not true.

Ten children stated that they still would like their parents to reconcile but have come to accept the irreversability of their parents' decision.

I want that to happen but it's almost, it's almost like cartoons. You can't run through a wall. Well that's, it's almost impossible for them too. Even if you wanted to run through a wall, you couldn't. Even if you wanted them to, they wouldn't want to.

Almost half the sample (30 out of 66) explicitly continued to hold on to the hope that the divorce would be a temporary phenomenon. A few made some reference to the unlikelihood of their parents getting back together but showed by later comments that they had not altogether abandoned this wish. Others straightforwardly asserted that they considered a reconciliation to be a real possibility. The wish was so strong that it commonly existed despite evidence, which the child may even have acknowledged, that the parents' current relationship was basically negative. Even the remarriage of one of the parents did not daunt the child's dreams.

Yeah, cause it hasn't been that long.

I'm still hoping they will. If they ever did then I think we'd be happier.

Just everytime someone, a man knocks at the door or something, I wish it was always my dad. And he'd say, "Hey, I'm sorry I got a divorce. I want to be married again."

The fantasies the children related sounded like the plots of TV movies. Common themes included the parents making up when they were thrown together by circumstances or the children, the father changing and realizing he missed his family, and a crisis such as an accident to one of the parents bringing them close together again.

Like when the mom or dad come and then drop him back at his home and stuff, they might get together again and stuff like that. They might be able to stand each other like that and then they might come back.

Dad doesn't have enough money and mom does and they get married again.

Well I used to dream that my father would go away and then he would come back and he was a changed person and he would love her and he would love us better and he'd just act real nice. And they'd be divorced and then a few years later he would come back and they would get married again.

Anger

At first I didn't understand about the divorce, why they wanted to get it, and then I was really angry at her.

The reactions discussed thus far were fairly easily addressed by the children. In contrast, anger was rarely mentioned spontaneously and appeared to cause considerable discomfort. Denial was evident to different degrees. A number of the youngsters did not mention that they had been (or were) angry until questioned directly but then referred to this reaction repeatedly throughout the remainder of the interview. Others denied having felt angry when first asked about it but revealed that they indeed felt this way in their responses to later questions such as "If your mom had to choose two things which she wished you didn't feel about the divorce or your dad, what would they be?" and "What might a mom do which would get her son/daughter really angry?" Some hedged a definite statement at all times:

> *Well I was sort of mad at my mom but not really. I was upset but I wasn't mad at her. I didn't want my dad to move away.*

However, when the entire interviews are examined it becomes obvious that anger was widely and intensely felt. In all, 61 out of the 66 children interviewed (92.4 percent) said that they had been angry at one or both parents about issues related to the divorce. The children did not typically clearly differentiate past anger from present anger but talked as if much of the anger was long lasting.

Even when the children were elaborate in their descriptions to the interviewer, 18 (27.2 percent of the children) claimed that they rarely, if ever, revealed their true feelings to their mother. Numerous reasons for covering up were provided: they were afraid of the parents becoming angry in return; they were afraid that their parents would stop loving them; they did not want their parents to think they did not love them anymore; they did not want to make their parents unhappy; they wanted to spare their parents further trouble; and they were afraid to let themselves really feel the intensity of their rage.

> C: *Just thinking in their mind, "Oh I wish mom didn't get divorced and I'm really mad about it but I don't want to say it."*
> I: And why wouldn't she want to say it?
> C: *Because she was afraid that her mom would do something or something like that, do something to her or talk to her or do something strict to her because she was mad that they got divorced.*
>
> *'Cause her parents went through alot and you know it would be easier for them if they didn't have an angry child or a child that's mad at them or something like that, and so to make it easier for the parents.*

> *Yes, maybe this person might feel that she's not loved anymore and she might run away then if someone found her and took her back she might get punished or something.*

The children explained their anger in several different ways. Frequently they stated that they were angry at their parents simply for getting a divorce.

> *Like how come you divorced and why can't you just like get together and not think about fighting.*

Given that they failed to see any reason which would justify such a drastic action, they were disgusted that their parents could not resolve their difficulties and continue living together. In attempting to understand why a separation was necessary, the children often attributed the responsibility for the decision to one parent. He/she then was blamed for the trouble and was the primary object of the child's anger.

> *Well just that your mom came to the decision and it's not fair.*

> *Well I was really mad at my mom. I just blew my top when she told me that because ... I just got mad because it was up to her.*

> *He thinks his mom's divorcing the dad when the dad didn't do something.... He'd be angry at the one that made the divorce.*

When the divorce was precipitated by the father's forming a relationship with another woman, he was usually considered to be totally at fault. More commonly however, as is evident in the quotes above, the mother is the child's chief target. As mentioned earlier, the children, with the exception of some preadolescent girls, exhibited a tendency to idealize their father. The anger they displayed towards their mother thus appears to result, in part, from a split in their ambivalence. Anger at their father is largely repressed while their mother is held responsible for causing all their pain. The nature of this split is undoubtedly connected to the child's need to hold onto a positive relationship with his father, a relationship which now feels far more shaky than the one he reinforces daily with his mother.

The parents' behavior during the divorce process and their relationship subsequent to it also was repeatedly reported as infuriating the children. They hated it when the parents continued to fight with each other.

> *Every time my dad picked us up to go over to his house, when my mom and dad started talking, they'd just get into an argument and then he gets all mad and my mom gets all mad and that just ruins the day.*

Because when they talk sometimes, the mom and the dad.... Like if he hangs up right when they're talking on the phone.

Arguments were especially resented if an attempt was made to involve the children.

[*The hardest thing he'll have to face is*] *if his dad is remarried and the mom gets remarried and they're fighting back and forth from their, well my mom and dad, my old mom and dad, they sometimes fight on the phone about things. They sometimes ask me questions about it and I don't want to get involved in it.*

Conversely, the youngsters were annoyed if the parents became so intent on dealing with their problems that they were made to feel left out. In general, becoming comfortable with the fact that their parents had to live apart had been a struggle and they did not want to keep witnessing how much they hated each other. Similarly, the parents' tendency to "bad-mouth" or "put down" each other was referred to very frequently as a major source of the children's upset and/or anger. (Mothers were cited more often in this regard but this is likely due to the fact that the children generally exhibited more conscious anger towards their mother as well as the interview's greater focus on the mother-child relationship.)

She felt my dad was just a big crock or something illegal and I didn't think so because I care about him.

[*A girl just wouldn't want to hear*] *that he always yelled at her and hit her or lied to her and made her really sick.*

She could like call my, or her kids' dad like a really dirty thing—like your dad went off and left me because he wanted to go out with younger ladies. Holler really mean things at the dad and the girl feels like her dad is not good.

[*A mom would upset her daughter when she*] *talks about her dad in bad ways. Like if your mother says your dad is a nasty, awful man. He goes out with other women and he has sex with them, other women. Your dad is a nasty man and that's like one of the things.*

The last two quotes were from girls age ten years, two months and nine years. They indicate the extent to which the children are informed of the details of the divorce and each parent's view of it. The children are clearly uncomfortable with being drawn into the marital conflict in this manner.

The children resented their mother for saying anything negative about their father even when they had already revealed that they shared many of the same thoughts. It was explained that it was okay for them to be angry at their father for ways he had disappointed them but they did not want to hear it from anyone else.

Well for some reason I don't like it when she's mad at him or something like that because, well it is his fault a little bit, I guess it is, I don't know if it's her fault or not but I don't like really her talking about him or him talking about her.

In keeping with their need not to hear anything negative about their father, none of the children commented at the anger at him for failing to visit frequently. Either out of a fear of alienating him further by expressing this anger or a fear of the pain which would accompany an acknowledgment of the degree of their disappointment, they dealt with this problem only indirectly. For example, a few children showed their dissatisfaction with their current relationship with their father by explaining that they were angry at him for having broken promises to them.

Well yeah, he promised me a few things and then I never got them and I was sort of angry, really angry.

When he'd tell me something, promise it to me and go and do it with his girlfriend.

Fears and Concerns

She wouldn't feel too good because if something happened to her mother, like she died in the night, then she wouldn't know what would happen to her. Like she might think she had to go to an orphanage or something and she might never see her dad again.

Divorce disturbs the certainty of children's lives and thus damages their trust in the predictability of their world. An examination of the children's responses to the interview reveals that they begin to have doubts about things formerly taken for granted. Most striking is their sudden questioning of their parents' commitment to caring for them. Additionally, they develop fears which were never a cause for concern before the divorce but which logically are no more likely to come true at present. Primarily, as is evident in the above quote, they become exceedingly afraid that their parents will be severely hurt or suddenly die.

A majority of the sample (37 out of 66 children) related that one of their earliest reactions to learning of the divorce was to become frightened that they would never see their father again or see him only rarely. The period of time until the father was settled into his new life and visitation was established on a regular basis was filled with anxiety. First of all, the children feared that their father's feelings toward them would change so that he would not want to see them. They interpreted his leaving home as his loving the entire family less and wondered whether their relationship with him was at an end.

> *... that I wouldn't see my dad again or he'd get killed in an automobile accident and die or something like that or, let me see, or that he might get married again and never want to talk to me or he might get mad at me and never want to talk to me. Something like that.*

Furthermore, they dreaded that they would not be informed of where he was living so that they could not contact him. Relatedly, they were afraid that he would move far away so that getting together would be very difficult.

> *I felt like they'd get separated all over the world or my dad would move somewhere and I wouldn't know where he lived.*

They also had concerns that their parents' animosity for each other would interfere with their ability to maintain a relationship with both parents.

> *Like it might just, the parent, their father might like, the parents might just hate each other so that the other one will move far away and then the mother will never know where the father is, you know, if it's the mother that kept the kids. So then they would never get to see their father again.*

Last, the children feared that something drastic would happen to their father so that he would be unable to visit them. This fear will be discussed in detail shortly.

In families where the father established himself in a house or apartment located near to the home of the children and initiated frequent contact with them, these fears were quickly abated. The concrete knowledge of a definite address and phone number, and the reassurance provided by regular visits, were found very comforting. When the father did move far away (five had moved out of state by the time the interview took place) or indeed seemed disinterested in the children, they felt that their fears were justified. However, the fear of losing the father does not appear ever truly to disappear. Almost all of the children whose father had remarried made a point of stating that when they were told of the upcoming marriage, they again became frightened that he would no longer want to see them.

Twenty-six children (39.4 percent of the sample) agreed that they were afraid that their mother would leave them too. Compared to the fear of totally losing the father, concerns about losing the mother do not appear to be as intense or central to the child's divorce experience. Whereas the fear discussed above was mentioned spontaneously by all the children listed, the fear of the mother walking out was only commented upon in response to a direct question, with three exceptions. Commonly, the children reasoned that if something unexpected, like the divorce, could occur and the father could move away, they had to be prepared for anything.

> *Sometimes they might because they think well, I never thought my mom and dad would ever go apart but they did and so, if they could, why couldn't my mom just suddenly leave.*

> *Oh yes, cause once one's gone, the other might go.*

> *Well she might think that since her father left, it might be because of her and her mother might go off and leave her too.*

With their father absent from the home (and in some cases relatively unavailable to them) the children felt especially dependent on their mother. In their view, her departure would force them to fend for themselves, a prospect they regarded as very scary.

> *Yeah, I guess he would really hope not because she's the only one left to go to.*

> *Yes, when she was out late at night to like a party or something and I was afraid that she'd never come back. She'd leave us alone and we'd have to go to some stupid old place.*

Interestingly, none of the children reached the conclusion that they would live with their father.

In addition to worrying that their parents will choose to discontinue their relationship with them, a large portion of the interviewed children were frightened that factors beyond the parents' control would cause all contact to cease. Despite the fact that this fear was not suggested by the interviewer, a list of the possible misfortunes mentioned by the children would be extensive and horrifying to consider. One eight-year-old boy had clearly thought of several possibilities:

You have bad dreams about your mom and dad or whoever it is that got divorced, hit by a car or something or got in a car accident, got ran over by something, got shot or something like that, got stabbed. They'd be worried about that 'cause they'd think it was really true.

The children also worried that a parent would get sick and die, get beaten up, get "raped and kidnapped," get "caught in jail" or need to be hospitalized for unspecified reasons. Unlike the previously discussed worry about losing their father, a fear of the parents being hurt and/or dying was still felt strongly in all cases.

Concerns about the mother's health and safety predominated: 7 children stated that they were worried about both parents, 6 just about their father, and 21 just about their mother (for a total of 51.5 percent of the sample). It appears that because the children live with their mother and their dependence on her for their daily survival is more obvious to them, the thought of something happening to her is more frightening. It is also possible that the children view their mother as more vulnerable to attack because their father is not present to protect her. The fear of something dreadful befalling their mother lies behind much of their reluctance to have her go out. Several children stated that they became frightened when their mother went out particularly when she did not tell them where she was going or came home late especially if she was later than expected.

Any time I would ask her what time are you coming home she goes, "I don't know." I go "couldn't you give me like a brief time." She goes "What are you, a cop?" I like to know what time she's coming home. Like if she's coming home like 11:00, to like know what time she was coming home. It would help me out.

Because the children are unable to see their father each day, they do not have the opportunity to reassure themselves that their fears have not become reality.

C: *When dad's gone I always, when he was around I always worried you know but I didn't worry that much 'cause I always knew he was around. And now that he's gone, I don't know where he's at or what he's doing or what trouble he might be in.*

I: What sort of trouble?

C: *Well, I always had the feeling that he was going to be hurt . . . and in the hospital or something like that. Or he was killed and I wouldn't know about it.*

With regard to both parents, these fears likely reflect frightening fantasies stimulated by the events the children have witnessed (e.g., the parents' fights) and their own unconscious responses to the divorce (e.g., a wish to punish the parents).

All the children who expressed fear about their parents getting hurt were also clearly revealing how vulnerable they felt themselves. Some stated this explicitly, moving quickly from describing their fear about their mother and/or father to wondering how they would manage on their own or with whom they would live.

> *Think her mother was sick or something and think that her father wasn't there to help her and if her mother died and she wouldn't have anybody and she wouldn't know where to go.*

Fear for themselves was also reflected in 16 children's concern (24.2 percent) about their mother's tension or depression. The children both felt bad that their mother was so upset and frightened of its effect on her ability to take care of them. Several children stated that they had been afraid that their mother would never recover from the divorce.

Concerns about their father's welfare and feelings appeared to be more completely altruistic. It seems that many children feel that since their mother is no longer interested in how their father is faring, they must take on the responsibility of looking out for him. Fourteen youngsters (21.2 percent) talked about their worry that their father would not eat well, would not find a nice place to live, and above all would be lonely and unhappy.

> *Sometimes I worry, most of the time I worry about him because there is this one man who is collecting something and I think it's bills and he went over to my dad's house but my dad was luckily not home. . . . I thought it was a bill collector 'cause right then my dad was flat broke. . . . I was wanting to live with my dad . . . because our dad didn't have nobody to cook for him or anything and care for him.*

> *Well my dad has a drinking [problem], he drinks a lot and when he's worried or misses somebody he drinks just a lot. . . . You just worry about him a lot.*

At about the same time that the children contemplated the prospect of losing their father, many reportedly also worried about other aspects of their future. Thirty-six children (54.5 percent) stated that when the separation first occurred they had worried about what their life would be like.

Yeah, the future and what his mom's going to do. Like if his mom is going to be mad or really nice with him, he would think about it. He would cry.

Scared? [I: What of?] *I don't know. I'd always lived with my mom and dad and it's sort of weird just living with one of them.*

I was pretty scared—scared of what it'd be like. Like what my dad would be like and what my mom would be like. And how it would be for me. Like if things would really change a lot.

I didn't know what had happened. Like what would happen to us. What we'd do and stuff.

Specific worries included wondering who would take care of them, whether they would be able to continue seeing their father's relatives, and whether they would need to move. Additionally, 11 children (16.6 percent) indicated that they had personalized their mother's fear about insufficient finances. They imagined dire consequences of her being unable to support them.

Well I had been living for most of the years, about eight, nine years of my life with two parents. I had been used to that and all of a sudden I had one parent and she didn't even have a job yet and I was scared where we were going to get the money, how we were going to survive and all this. I just didn't know quite what to think.

Afraid, like when my mom first got the house and paid all the bills, I didn't think we'd be able to keep the house. I was afraid we were going to get kicked out of our house. . . . I was afraid that our money would run out and we wouldn't have enough money and we couldn't buy new clothes and people would tease me, can't afford to do things and stuff like that.

The Pressures of Having Divorced Parents

It's just another day but you feel more mature because you feel that you can do without that one parent. You still miss him but you just feel you can do without him.

Alongside the children's intensified sense of vulnerability and dependence on their mother was an increased awareness of their own capabilities. Almost half of the sample (8 spontaneously, 23 when questioned, for a total of 46.9 percent of those interviewed) revealed that they had felt pressured to act suddenly more mature following the separation. This reaction was reported far more often by the older child of the sibling pair (i.e., in families where two children were interviewed this reaction was related by both children five times, the oldest child 10 times and the youngest child two times; in families where only one child was interviewed, this reaction was noted by the oldest child seven times and the youngest child two times), implying that mothers are more likely to make greater maturity demands on their first child as a result of the divorce. Alternatively, the older sibling may himself decide that he needs to assume more responsibility in order to fill the gap left by the absent parent.

Much of the time, the issue of feeling grownup was addressed in terms of the new chores which the child must accomplish. The children stated that they felt like a second adult, explaining that they now shared the daily family tasks with their mother. Some specified which parent they were in part replacing:

Like being the grown man and taking responsibility around the house.

Well you kind of feel like a grownup, like you're another lady living with her because she lets you do extra special jobs and special things that your dad used to do.

I felt like I was, you know like I was getting the divorce instead of my mom because I had to take over all of the household, I had to take it over. My mom was, she was the breadwinner in the family. I was like the mother and she was the father.

Additionally several older children indicated that they babysat for their younger sibling more frequently than they had before the divorce. At times, the children appeared to have begun actually to think of themselves as a parent to their sister or brother.

I try to keep [my brother] in line so he won't go wild and stuff. My mom used to do that and now I do it.

The practice of watching out for the younger sibling occasionally extended to looking out for mom's interest as well . Some children seemed especially sensitive to the pressures their mother was under and made every attempt to make her life easier. For example, they straightened up the house so that she might relax when she got home. In general they tried to spare her and worked at not doing anything which would upset her.

He has to watch out for his brother and he has to take out the garbage and everything. And he has to take care of everybody mostly.

Well somebody else isn't there so you got to act more grownup and, just be better to your parents—just be nicer and if they ask you to do something, do that.

Another aspect of the children's sense that they had immediately to mature a great deal when their parents separated was the fact that they were required to spend more time unsupervised. They explained that they had to learn to be comfortable being home by themselves and to do things on their own for which they formerly depended on one of their parents.

I just had to grow up a lot, really kind of, my mom had to work and she's working in real estate so she was gone a lot so I had to adjust to that and just kind of grow up and become more independent.

Their new more mature status was regarded as a mixed achievement. The children enjoyed their mother's greater reliance on them and their consequent image of themselves as little adults. However, at times they viewed their many responsibilities and the need to be self-reliant as a burden.

I've had to do a lot of work. My sister is really a big pain. I clean up the house and she makes a bigger mess and I don't like it. . . . [When mother went back to work] I didn't like it because during the summer I had to watch my sister and it was sort of hard. I couldn't go over to my friend's house and stuff like that.

Sometimes it's kind of fun, to be able to do things that my mom usually does. And then in some ways you get kind of tired of it because my mom's always asking me to do things and I want to do something else.

[A boy would feel grown up about] a lot 'cause he'd be alone sometimes when his mom left him and think he's big but he wouldn't really be big, he'd be pretty little.

Positive Reactions

I almost cried for days and days but finally I forgot about it and I just thought of something happy—like my mom and dad won't fight anymore because my dad's not going to be there. And we won't have all this yelling and screaming.

Positive reactions were largely absent from the children's divorce experience. When they existed, as is illustrated by an eight-year-old girl above, they were described as a bright spot in an otherwise unhappy situation. Thirty-eight children (57.6 percent of those interviewed) were able when asked (no one mentioned this reaction spontaneously), to discuss some positive aspect to their parents getting a divorce but they rarely devoted more than a couple of sentences per interview to the topic. The remaining children could think of nothing positive to say.

Most frequently, the children communicated that they had been relieved that arguments and/or physical fights would stop. Mainly, these 20 children just disliked seeing their parents hurt each other (emotionally and physically). A few said that they were glad no longer to get caught in the middle of battles. However, it was explained that their relief was not equated to thinking that divorce was a good idea. This is evident in a ten-and-one-half-year-old's response to being asked if she ever felt relieved:

> *I did in a way because I didn't like every night to hear a fight and stuff. And I thought like maybe it would be for two days or something but not like three years.*

Six children related that they were pleased because their relationship with their father had improved since the divorce. Positive changes included his becoming "nicer," "less grumpy," and "less bossy." An additional six children commented that they were "relieved" and/or "happy" when the divorce became final. They felt glad that the tension connected to the divorce proceedings could abate and that their mother would become generally calmer as a result.

> *I mean it was sad when it happened but I was sort of glad that they signed the papers and everything. It wasn't as nerve-wracking.*

Although the children were emphatic in their assertion that they were not happy about their parents separating, most made clear that they were also not devastated by the divorce. After the initial intense reaction, negative feelings certainly continued (to different degrees as noted earlier) but life went on as usual too. The typical ups and downs with friends and between family members occurred similar to before the divorce.

> *See I don't really talk to my mother much about the divorce. All I really talk to her about is what happened in school and stuff like that. And if my brother did something to me like hit me with one of his combs or something.*

> *[I want to tell other kids] they're not going to have a very pleasant time while they're divorced because it's not fun and you don't see him that often but everything will be alright.*

6

The Children's Responses— The Mothers' Views

Despite the mothers' obviously greater maturity, their ability to relate their children's reactions to the divorce varied in much the same way as the children's descriptions of them. Slightly over 15 percent of the women accepted all of the children's behavior at face value without ever even considering the possibility that the children were either covering up certain reactions or expressing some feelings indirectly. For instance, they accepted the children's outward calm as evidence that they had no difficulty accepting the divorce. Moreover, a child's increased unruliness was seen as simply that—increased unruliness. The mother might conclude that the child would not "get away" with this behavior if the father was present but did not take the step to connect this negativism with the divorce itself. On the other hand, approximately 16 percent of the mothers were extremely attuned to their child's feelings, describing both reactions which were transparently present and those which the child had trouble revealing directly. Some of these women related that they believed they had been insensitive to the children's reactions around the time of the separation due to their own emotional turmoil during that period but were now making a greater effort to understand the children's feelings.

   The family style of coping was evident in the manner in which the mother decided on her responses to the interview. One group of women based their statements largely on what had been told them by the children during discussions specifically focusing on the divorce. Others similarly determined how their child felt from what he had verbalized or demonstrated by his actions. A third group however, indicated that they had rarely, if ever, talked about the divorce with their children. They assumed what the child must have felt by using their knowledge of their child's personality or simply by putting themselves in their child's shoes and imagining how he must have reacted. They insisted that few reactions were actually noticed. Some of this latter group had never really considered these issues before the interview.

I guess I've tried to assess their feelings before but I've never gone into it step by step like you have. It just wouldn't occur to me that way. I would hope that these things that happened to a large degree would not be bad for them for I certainly would never do anything to hurt them willingly and if I have, I will feel very badly about it.

A few women replied in the negative to almost all of the questions regarding whether they thought their child had ever experienced a certain reaction to the divorce although the interview occasionally raised doubts in their mind about this view. Some reactions were apparent in other contexts later in the interview but not recognized as such by the mothers. Some women were very defensive in reporting their children's reactions, repeatedly needing to assert that their children's responses to the divorce process were mild and normal. Others straightforwardly communicated that the aftermath of the separation had been terrible but that the family as a whole was functioning much better at present or that the children's upset had lessened considerably.

This chapter focuses on the mothers' view of those children included in the child sample. In cases where one of the siblings in a family was older or younger than the targeted age range, their comments on just one child will be examined.

Surprise

They didn't know what to do. They just totally went into shock and they would not talk for awhile. And they would have lots of questions. . . . just checking out, like what in the world are you doing, why, like I just, everybody else's parents seemed to be going through this but I didn't think we ever would.

On the whole, mothers do not recognize the degree to which their children are surprised by the divorce. Whereas almost 91 percent of the children interviewed commented that the divorce had been unexpected, only 15 out of 40 women (i.e., 37.5 percent) thought that this was so. Furthermore, four of these mothers stated that just their younger child was surprised. Frequently mothers made a connection which appeared to be absent from the children's logic—they assumed that the child's awareness of tension between the parents was tantamount to his considering divorce as a possibility. Even if the child would agree with the parent's former assertion, it has already been stressed that this equation is not commonly made by children.

The mothers who described their children as having been surprised noted, in parallel fashion to the children's comments, both the shock which accompanied the news of the impending divorce and the surprise that it actually took place. The mothers attributed their child's surprise variously to their belief that "no one had any inkling" that a marital breakup was brewing including the mother herself, the parents' efforts to keep the marriage problems hidden from the children, and the children's refusal to acknowledge problems that the mother regarded as obvious (e.g., "I think they had just ignored all that had gone on"). Six mothers talked about their children's failure to believe that their father would not return home and the divorce plans would not be cancelled.

Dana ran to her room and wanted to be alone and circled on her calendar the date that he said that we were going to talk about it. She circled it and she wrote "Daddy comes home." So that was her reaction—he was going away, like to some convention or something and he was coming home that day, so she really didn't."

Confusion

She felt very bad about it. She didn't understand. She really didn't understand why it had to be done.

Fewer mothers observed that their children were confused by some aspect of the divorce process than the children indicated in their interviews. The discrepancy between the mothers' and children's reports however was not as great as for "surprise." Eighteen mothers referring to 29 children (43.9 percent of the child sample), as opposed to 37 children (56 percent) discussing themselves, mentioned this reaction. The mothers' greatest misreading of the children involved their believing that they contributed to the ending of the marriage (i.e., only four women regarding five children as compared to 14 children). The women seemed erroneously to assume that their explanation of why the divorce was necessary and/or their inclusion of a statement that the child was not at fault would serve to alleviate this concern totally. Seven mothers recognized that their offspring did not comprehend why the divorce was necessary. Certain actions or comments of the parents were suggested as adding to the child's confusion. For example, one mother pointed out that the children did not find the father's assertion that he still loved the mother to make sense. Another mentioned that the children could not understand why she and her ex-husband could be friendly to each other but still not want to live together.

Five mothers discussed their children's difficulty understanding what the divorce would mean in terms of the actual impact on their family situation. Again, the mothers accepted blame for some of this confusion, believing that a time lag between when the children were informed of the divorce and when the parents' marital relationship was truly terminated or the father moved out for good, complicated any explanation.

Sadness

> *They were just floored, heartbroken. They cried, very upset. It was something that they just didn't expect.*

With one exception, the mothers' reports matched the children's in their conclusion that children are distressed by the divorce experience. Some mothers seemed to underestimate severely the duration of their children's unhappiness, asserting that they felt totally fine a day or a month after being told of the divorce (e.g., "They forgive and forget so easily") but most recognized that some sadness lingered for a great deal longer. Very few however, realized that their children might currently still be upset by thoughts of the divorce.

In describing their children's reaction to the divorce process, the mothers fleshed out the picture of sadness related by the children. In addition to indicating that the children became extremely upset when first informed of the separation, often crying themselves to sleep that night, they explained that crying spells were common in the next several months. The children reportedly became unusually sensitive so that they were easily hurt, insulted or irritated. The children therefore, not only cried when the issue of the divorce was raised in some way but whenever anything did not go just right. In some cases, unhappiness about the separation was only evident in an indirect manner.

> *Craig was more whining when stuff was going on or else he would break into tears. That's the other thing he did. At just the slightest sharpness in somebody's voice and he would just sort of absolutely fall apart and fill with tears. He was very thin-skinned for awhile.*

> *Robin always has reacted to things with tears and upset and moody and that kind of thing for a day and Elise sort of doesn't react for awhile. It might show in negative behavior or some aggression or in something else. She sometimes will not ever shed tears. And then they'll come out later. Maybe something will go wrong at school and she'll come home crying and when she tells me about what went on at school, she'll also tell me about her daddy being gone, so that's the way it comes out in her.*

A common notion communicated in many adult interviews was that one of the children was closer to his father so that the loss was greater for him and he was consequently more upset than his sibling. This belief was not referred to by the children. On the other hand, the women missed the connection made by the children between regular frequent visitation and a quicker recovery from the anguish caused by the separation. In general, although the large majority of mothers certainly recognized that the departure of the father caused the children pain they, unlike the children, contended that he had little impact on their overall well being.

The mothers typically commented that the children's moods depended on how the mother was feeling. Some women regarded their behavior as the chief determinant of the children's reactions, assuming that once they were relaxed and happy about the divorce, the children felt similarly.

Depression

> *My daughter went through a stage of depression. She got very quiet and mopey.... She'd stay in her room. She'd read a lot. If you asked her to do something that she didn't feel she wanted to do, she just wouldn't say anything. She wouldn't move.... She doesn't have hardly any friends...where she used to have a lot of friends and then all of a sudden...*

While the mothers were not generally cognizant of the pain the divorce still caused their children, a substantial group presented the children as having considerable difficulty coping in the period following the separation. In addition to describing their children's profound sadness, 15 women (37.5 percent of those interviewed) detailed several other symptoms of an underlying depression. Typically, these symptoms were reported to have persisted for approximately a year. Although all but one of these mothers referred to just one child in the sample, the total number of children believed to be depressed (24.2 percent) is still greater than was explicitly indicated in the child interviews.

The mothers believed that the divorce had temporarily severely impaired the children's normal functioning. Interactions with peers as well as with family members were sharply affected. The children reportedly lost interest in socializing and pulled away from friends. Activity levels in general were severely reduced. At home the youngsters became more quiet, at times to the extent of refusing to talk about anything. Younger children were commonly perceived as becoming clingier. The older children in the sample however, more often withdrew from their mother and sibling. They were described as retreating to their room and reading or watching television for hours. The above behaviors were sometimes linked with poor concentration in school and a decline in school performance during the year following the separation.

The mothers, on the whole, placed less emphasis than the children on the problem of low self-esteem. Thirty-seven children stated that they had been uncomfortable with friends following the divorce because they felt "different" or less worthy but only 20 children (30.3 percent) were observed by their mother to have felt this way. Furthermore, most of the mothers who agreed that this reaction existed, did not think to discuss it until the interviewer asked about it specifically (14 mothers in total, nine in response to a direct question) and then did not realize its intensity. The women thus seemed quite attuned to the possibility of depression in the immediate aftermath of the separation but were relatively unaware of the divorce's long-term impact on their children's self-image.

When the mothers talked of the children's discomfort with peers they reiterated the issues raised by the children in their interviews. They understood that their children were embarrassed because they felt different from other children. Commonly, it was noted that they were the only one of their friends "without two parents."

It was like he was ashamed that that kid had a dad and he didn't, living in the house.

School was seen as emphasizing this difference because of the orientation of forms and special events to two parents living together. The mothers also explained that their children felt "somehow less" because their father did not live with them. Playmates were believed to increase the youngsters' sense of loss because of their references to their father's easy availability. The women usually attributed their children's discomfort to doubts about their self-worth but generally failed to regard this as a more broad-based problem which affected all aspects of functioning.

Missing Dad

She missed him because he wasn't there at night, that kind of thing. Just because he wasn't there.

Although the mothers again described this reaction as less intense and of briefer duration than the children reported, their discussion of the reasons the children missed their father and the way this feeling was manifested was similar to that offered in the child interviews. Most of the 31 mothers who mentioned this reaction (five referring to only one of their two children; 11 from families in which only one child was interviewed for a total of 69.7 percent of the child sample), focused on the children's wish that their father was home with them. The women realized that they missed his daily presence and discussed the children's desire to see him, or at least talk to him, frequently. Weekend visits were reportedly eagerly awaited by much of the sample. When particular aspects of the father-child relationship were specified, they usually involved the typical day-to-day activities of parenting. The mothers sensed the loss their children experienced by not being able to share the "little things" with their father.

Going on trips or just weekend campouts, or Girl Scout dinners, school affairs, bringing home papers. It was important to the kids to bring things home and have their dad look at it and pin it up on the bulletin board. Everyday things like that that's the hardest thing. . . . He doesn't think to take them for little things, like he used to just come and take Brenda and Gwen for root beer or out to feed the ducks or just all the little things that you just take for granted in everyday life. He doesn't feel that they're important now. If he does something, I guess he feels he's got to do some big drastic thing, like take them to Cedar Point or something.

She was closer to her dad so she had to learn to do without a lot of things that she used to do. Although for a period of time when he was still around, he took them out to eat on Thursday nights and he would go see them on Saturday or Sunday afternoons, but she used to just kind of tag along when he would be mowing the lawn or working in the garden or something, she would be with him. And he did not come over here to see the children and spend time here with them, so all the times that they would be doing things with him was kind of false parenting situations where they would go to a shopping mall or MacDonald's or you know, they weren't the kind of activities she'd ever done with him before, so she missed that kind of thing.

As is clear in the above quotes, the mothers did not think that their ex-husbands were aware of what the children missed or that visits were able to satisfy the children's needs.

Some mothers talked about the various roles the father had played in the family and how the children felt a gap since these roles were vacated. The children were seen as missing the father as ally, as buffer between themselves and their mother when she was angry or unreasonable, as playmate (especially for roughhousing and joking around) and as substitute when the mother was busy.

On the whole, the women were very insightful regarding the realistic aspects of the children's missing their father. They showed little understanding however, of the children's idealization of the predivorce relationship with their father or how this contributed to the intensity of their longing for him. When the children expressed their idealized views openly, the mothers were resentful; when the children kept their feelings more hidden, the mothers assumed that the father's importance had dwindled.

Missing the Parental Couple or the Predivorce Family

Perhaps because the mothers needed to believe for their own defensive reasons that the family functioned as well now as before the divorce and that the children shared this view, or because they had long since ceased thinking of themselves as part of a couple with their ex-husband, the women on the whole did not recognize that the children missed the parents as a couple. The desire of the children to have both parents in the same place at the same time was apparently not witnessed. Most mothers also did not realize that the children missed them when they were with their father, possibly assuming that since the children wanted so much to see their father they did not feel bad about leaving their mother behind. Alternatively, many mothers were so envious of the father's ability to use his time with the children as "fun time" they failed to consider that the children did not value this time more highly than weekday time with their mother. Only 5 mothers made any reference to the children missing the parental couple or the predivorce family.

Loneliness

> Oh I'm sure they were. They get lonely for him. They'll ask is he going to pick us up this weekend. I know they're lonely, period, because I should be spending more time with them, but you know, it's just a bad thing, like I had to go to work and like I mentioned before, work has really helped me in a lot of ways because I've made friends at work, and I felt lonely but now I have work to look forward to, but then you know it's always got to be taken into the kids' time, the time that you'd ordinarily give them you have to. . . .

Although over three-fourths of the women realized that their children missed their father, they did not typically perceive the loss of the father as contributing to the children's loneliness. Rather they connected this reaction chiefly to their own inability to spend as much time with the children as they did prior to the divorce. Work in particular, was seen as interfering with treasured parts of the mother-child relationship including getting the children ready for school, having lunch with them during their midday break and being there when they returned home from school. Twenty-four mothers (60 percent of the sample) thought that their children felt lonely following the separation. Eight mothers focused on the effects of their absence exclusively.

When the women interpreted their children's loneliness as resulting from the absence of a father as well as the increased unavailability of a mother, they spoke in terms of the children missing the presence of a father figure. Usually these mothers did not link the loneliness with the children missing *their* father but rather with them losing out because there was no man or simply a second adult available. It was not uncommon for a woman to state that even though her husband had done very little for the children, she realized that he was still another person to talk to or play with while she was occupied with household responsibilities or attending to one of the other children.

Hope of Reconciliation

It was really hard telling the children that we were going to get a divorce. They both cried and they obviously—two things—one was they felt guilty that it was their fault and the other was they wanted us to get back together and any signs that we were really friendly with each other and stuff they would think oh good, maybe they're going to get back together. And of course there was this long period of several months where that was hard to watch.

Other than sadness, mothers reported the children's hope that the parents would reconcile more frequently than any other reaction experienced during the divorce process. Thirty-six out of 40 mothers (90 percent) stated that their children clearly revealed their wish that their parents would get back together and in some cases attempted to bring this about. The total of children concerned almost duplicates the number of children who commented in their interview that they had wanted this to occur: 54 children discussed by the mothers compared to 56 children discussing themselves.

The major difference between the reports of the mothers and those of the children regarded the time frame for this reaction. Almost all of the children had indicated that they still wished for a reconciliation; 30 continued to believe it was a viable possibility. The mothers on the other hand failed to recognize the tenacity with which the children held this dream. Of the mothers who specified the duration of this reaction, only 10 (speaking about 16 children) believed that their children currently held onto the hope that the divorce would be temporary. Six more (discussing eight children) stated that their children still wanted their parents to get back together but realized that this was impossible. Fourteen women however, referring to 21 children, commented that their children had hoped for a reconciliation at one time but no longer did so. All of these women stated that their children had totally accepted the divorce by the time it was final (i.e., six months to one and-one-half years from the time of filing).

I don't think they thought anything about it after that.

Often, the time span of this reaction was considered to be much shorter; estimates typically ranged from a day to several months.

The discrepancy between the mothers' and children's view of this reaction appears to stem from several sources. A major reason that the mothers decide that the children no longer think about them getting back together with their ex-husband is that the children stop questioning them about it. It seems likely that after numerous disappointing responses from their parents, the children start keeping their dreams a secret. In this way, pain of finding out once again that they are unrealistic is avoided. The mothers, in turn, usually find it difficult to cope with the children's repeated requests for a parental reconciliation (either because they share the child's unattainable fantasies or because the child's wishes are totally at odds with their own goals) and are only too glad to have this sort of reaction cease. They are thus unlikely to probe to discover if this feeling has simply been covered up. Moreover, given that they are beginning to feel (or have always felt) that the divorce was for the best, they assume the children's feelings are moving in a similar direction.

Anger

> *Sure there was some resentment there. I think that would be only natural because I really disrupted their lives.*

> *Yes in the beginning they were very upset with him and even now they get very angry with him. Like in the beginning because he's found another woman and left them for this other person and now because he doesn't come to get them when he promises to and doesn't do as many things with them as they'd like.*

While the majority of women observed that their children had been (or were still) angry to some extent at both parents, the issues related to each parent were discussed separately. It was rare for the women to conceptualize their children's anger as being directed at them as a couple for such things as being unable to resolve their differences in a way that would allow them to remain married. Thirty-four out of the 40 interviewed women (85 percent) reported that at least one of their children had experienced anger because of the divorce but only five (12.5 percent) thought of this reaction in the way just described. Moreover, a substantial group of women viewed their children as angry at only one parent. Two contrasting scenarios were depicted. In families where the mother believed that she was the sole object of her children's antagonism, she felt maligned. The children's anger was seen as stemming mainly from current disappointments with their father but he allegedly was spared its expression. While the children were furious with their mother, the father was regarded as if he could do no wrong. In other cases, the mother described the children as her chief supports. They shared her hurt and were angry at their father for causing the family pain. The mother in turn, was viewed as a passive victim who certainly deserved no negative feelings. In both situations, the mothers clearly picked up on the children's split in ambivalence but did not usually consider the defensive reasons for the one-sided feelings they witnessed.

As is demonstrated in the two quotes which opened this section, the mothers shared the children's tendency to assign blame to one person. From the mothers' interviews it is clear that children are commonly informed of which parent filed for the divorce. It was the mothers' assumption that this parent alone was the target of the children's anger concerning the divorce itself.

The mothers echoed the numerous postdivorce parental behaviors which the children had said infuriated them. Most frequently, they related that their children became angry and upset if they criticized their ex-husband in any way or showed that they were angry at him. Some knew this to be true with regards to their husband's actions as well. Unlike the reports in the previous chapter, several mothers commented that their children were angry at their father for not visiting them regularly and in general, removing himself from the children's daily life. It appears that what the children discussed in terms of sadness and fear, the mothers saw as anger.

Fears and Concerns

I think first of all there's an insecurity—that something that's normal, a normality to them, a family with two parents and stuff was disrupted and then—now what happens? They don't have the background or experience to see that other families can function normally, so they can't imagine that they can because it's like they lost an arm and they don't know what to do without that arm. It doesn't make any difference how much that arm participated in their lives, but that's what everybody else has.

In the same way that the children did not realize that mothers experienced many fears related to the divorce, the mothers as a whole were not cognizant of the variety or intensity of the children's fears. It seems that both groups viewed the other as more secure and relaxed with their situation than they described themselves.

More than half the children commented that they had worried that their father would completely disappear when he left home. In contrast, 13 mothers, discussing 21 children (i.e., slightly less than one-third of the sample), noted their children's fear of not seeing their father again. However, the content of these mothers' statements was very much like that of the children's. The women explained that their children had asked numerous questions when the separation was initiated as to the whereabouts of their father's new residence and the frequency of visitation, revealing their anxiety. Several mothers believed that their children's upset when informed of the divorce was primarily due to this fear about losing their father. They contended that their worry quickly abated once they had been reassured he would continue to be involved in their lives. Although mothers commonly thought that their children felt their father did not love them as much as he had before the divorce, this feeling was rarely connected to their having been afraid of losing him. The mothers typically saw their children as reacting mainly to the reality of their situation, not to their fantasies about what the future would bring. If the fathers were inattentive, the children were hurt. If the fathers visited regularly, the children were secure in their relationship with him.

In keeping with the mothers' tendency to stress their role in the children's reactions, the number of women (19 in all) who agreed that the children were nervous that they would copy the fathers and leave too was the largest group to discuss a specific fear. In addition to the reluctance to have their mothers go anyplace alone, clinginess, intensive questioning about the itinerary and time schedule for their evening or weekend away from home, and frequent checking that they were still around were cited as evidence that this fear existed.

> *They were afraid that I was going to leave too, I think. . . . In the mornings they'd come into my room and check if I was still there. . . . They were always on me, big hugs and everything when I was going somewhere like I would never return. I think they still had this little fear that I wasn't coming back.*

> *Oh yes. Or if maybe I did go out for an evening or something she would want to know if she could stay up until I got home and when I was coming home, what I was going to do, where I was going to go. She just wanted to be sure.*

Many of the mothers felt that only their younger children were worried about them leaving (bringing the total of children concerned to 23). They based their decision on the fact that he/she was the one to demonstrate the behavior described above. Younger children were not more highly represented in the group that claimed to have experienced this fear when the children described their own reactions.

At times the child's fear was evident in the mother's descriptions of certain incidents but she seemed oblivious to the possibility that he/she might be worried. For example, one woman related that she had on a particular occasion been away from home for two nights on business and then arranged to go out on a date the third night after working all day. She had been feeling slightly guilty thinking she may have been catering to herself a little too much but reported that she was promptly reassured when her son greeted her by saying, "You're the best mom in the world." This greeting was taken as proof that she was feeling bad and guilty for nothing—her kids hadn't minded at all. The idea that her son was worried about her absence and trying to bolster their relationship or make it more pleasant for her to stay home was not considered.

The most striking discrepancy between the reports of the children and the mothers concerned the fear of the parents getting hurt. Over half of the children had spontaneously mentioned their dread of something terrible befalling their parents, especially their mother, but only 4 women (discussing 4 children, 6 percent of the sample) picked up on this. It seems likely that the numbers would be somewhat higher if the interviewer had focused specifically on this fear as she did on concerns about the mother leaving home. Clearly much of the children's behavior elaborated to support the existence of the fear just examined, also, or more accurately, related to the worry that the parents would be lost because of some unexpected misfortune. However, the exceedingly small number of mothers to report this fear indicates that an important aspect of the child's divorce experience is not understood.

Whereas the 16 children who expressed worry about their mother's depression seemed to be doing so out of a mixture of selfish and altruistic concerns, the mothers who stated that their children were worried about them saw the children's reaction as totally supportive. These eight mothers explained that their children were very protective of them. They knew their mother had been hurt and tried to make sure this would not happen again. When aware that their mother was feeling down, they set to work at cheering her up.

Besides concerns regarding their parents, 15 mothers said that at least one of their children (22 in total) were worried about what their future would bring. Usually this fear was described in a vague way—the children were experiencing something new and upsetting, and were worried about what was going to happen to them. Moving to a new house was the most frequently cited specific change which the children dreaded. Only one mother, in contrast to 11 children, reported that financial worries contributed to the child's concern about his future.

The Pressures of Having Divorced Parents

John seemed to grow up fast and he considered himself the man of the house.... He would get a job, pick up a paper route. He could make money and help out. He wanted to help with anything and everything.

In contrast to most of the reactions discussed previously, mothers believed that their children were affected by the pressures created by the single-parent situation more frequently than this was reported by the children. For example, 24 mothers referring to 39 children (59 percent of the child sample), as compared with 31 children (47 percent), contended that their children acted in a more adult fashion since the divorce. The increase in the number of mothers citing this particular change was due to the fact that several women who viewed their children as having only minimal reactions to the divorce itself, nevertheless saw them as changing quite a bit in response to their new living situation. As was the case with the children, the mothers were more likely to see the older sibling as maturing rapidly rather than the younger but the majority of the mothers who commented on this reaction felt that both children had grown up in some way due to the divorce. A phenomenon observed by seven mothers but not mentioned at all by the children was for the son, when the children were of both sexes, or the older son, when there were two boys in the family, to become "the man of the house." This sort of role change accounted for the couple of cases in which only the younger child was seen as becoming more adult. Usually, the mothers encouraged their son's new image of himself but in a couple of instances they felt his increased sense of his own authority to be problematic. The explanation of how the boy acted differently typically involved his voluntarily taking on the chores such as the yardwork which had formerly been carried out by his father. Several boys were also described as becoming protective of their mother, overseeing her activities and trying to prevent her from getting hurt either by her ex-husband or current boyfriends.

Like the children, the mothers emphasized the practical aspects of this reaction such as the children's greater role in the upkeep of the house. Seventeen mothers stated that the greater time pressure on them required that the children accept more of the household responsibilities. In general, the children seemed to take on the tasks formerly accomplished by the same sex parent.

Seven women related that their children were, of necessity, on their own a great deal more than before the separation. The need to adjust to being without an adult and the consequent realization that this independence could be handled was observed to result in greater maturity. Also because of the mothers' greater number of hours away from home, six mothers said that their older child had to take on the responsibility of being the oldest one at home, which most often translated into watching out for the younger sibling.

Positive Reactions

Michael was just very unsure of himself as a person and his father was probably harder on him. He is very sensitive to verbal criticism and it has a real definite effect on him and he had no self-confidence. He didn't have a very good image of himself because his dad would say, "you're dumb, you're stupid, you can't do anything right" and he was firmly convinced of that. He couldn't believe that people liked him for what he was and his grades were, well they were Bs and Cs. Last year which was the first year that we were really alone all year long, he was on the honor roll. He did some things on his own. He found out that people liked him just for being him and his self-confidence has improved about 100 percent.

Given that the mothers, in comparison to the children, seemed in many ways to downplay the children's reaction to the divorce process, it is noteworthy that the number of children considered by the mothers to have positive reactions to this experience was exactly the same as the total of children who reported likewise. Furthermore, almost one-half of the 27 mothers concerned concentrated, as had the children, on the relief the children felt because fighting and/or hostile conditions had ended. However, while most of the above group of mothers viewed the children's relief as only a small part of their reaction to the separation, eight women observed a significant change for the better in their children. Primarily, they discussed how their children were altogether more relaxed and easy going since the divorce. Some mothers attributed this improvement simply to the ending of tension in the family. Most stated that it resulted from the departure of the father. The mothers explained that the father was either generally a hard person with whom to live for everyone or else had a particularly problematic relationship with one of the children. He was typically described as extremely and unfairly critical or easily angered. The pressure under which he placed the child was thus lifted when he no longer interacted with the family on a daily basis.

7

Another Look at Earlier Studies

Given the paucity of systematic studies in this field, particularly with normal populations, one goal of this research was to substantiate or bring into question the conclusions of previous research and theoretical writings. This chapter is therefore devoted to a comparison of the findings of the current research (as elaborated in the previous two chapters) with earlier work on children's responses to divorce.

Children's View of Their Own Reactions

The findings on children are examined mainly with regard to the major researchers in this field, Wallerstein and Kelly. In their initial reports (Wallerstein and Kelly, 1976; Kelly and Wallerstein, 1976) Wallerstein and Kelly talked of how the younger latency-age children were more immobilized by their feelings at the time of the separation, finding it difficult to get relief. The older latency and preadolescent group was described as being able to understand quickly and accept the reality. Defenses against disorganization were considered successful. Observations made at the time of the follow up interviews however (Wallerstein and Kelly, 1980), revealed that in the long run, a large portion of the older group did not cope nearly as well as initially indicated. The long-term perspective gained at the time of follow up is given support by the current children's interviews. In general, there is evidence that the older children's original outward appearance of understanding and acceptance was deceiving. In keeping with this discovery is the finding that, in several instances, the reactions which Wallerstein and Kelly linked only with the younger latency group are applicable to many of the older children as well. This last finding results in some disagreement between the two studies about how common a particular reaction is for this age group.

Despite the above differences, much of the conclusions of Wallerstein and Kelly is repeated here. This research adds to their work by expanding upon their explanations of certain reactions. Additionally, a detailed long-range perspective is provided for reactions other than the two concentrated upon by Wallerstein and Kelly, namely depression and anger. Finally, a few reactions, not discussed by Wallerstein and Kelly, are shown to be important.

Surprise

Landis (1960), Anthony (1974), and Toomin (1974) stated that children usually consider their predivorce home to have been happy and/or secure so that the divorce is not anticipated. There is little recognition of this commonly held notion by most writers before the research of Wallerstein and Kelly. Yet 60 out of the 66 children interviewed for this study revealed that they were surprised by the news of the divorce. Moreover, the children in this sample stressed the importance of their unpreparedness in their overall feelings at the time of the separation in a way not done in previous literature.

Confusion

Prior to this study, no one has truly discussed the confusion which children experience when their parents decide to divorce. Confusion was not mentioned by any of the authors cited when the list of expected reactions was presented in the literature review for this book. Wallerstein and Kelly (1976; Kelly and Wallerstein, 1976) talked of reactions such as disbelief and fear which may relate to confusion but did not refer to it specifically. In fact, as stated earlier, when discussing the older latency group, they asserted that the children quickly perceived the reality. The findings of this study suggest otherwise. Over half of the sample elaborated their confusion without any hints from the interviewer. While latency-age and preadolescent children may grasp the situation more easily than a younger child, they still do not really comprehend the chain of events. A quarter of the children were even confused to the point that they did not understand what was physically to take place. The children's reports indicate that parents' comments and behavior often add to the confusion rather than diminishing it. Furthermore, although this reaction only pertains to a minority of the sample, a larger number of children expressed self-blame and showed its persistence than would be expected based on the summary of Wallerstein and Kelly.

In addition to confusion stemming from an immature understanding of the complexity of a marital relationship and the legal steps leading to its dissolution, the confusion elaborated by the children likely results from a view of their parents which does not allow for weaknesses or marital conflict. The children's sense of security is believed to be dependent on their family continuing to exist as it always has and thus on the perception of the parents as stable, in control, and content with their life. Defenses against altering this view are strong even when strong evidence to the contrary is presented. Parents, in their efforts to maintain the children's sense of security and positive outlook, often feed into this defensive structure by hiding their problems or reassuring the child that all is well. When the divorce is inevitable, children must then radically shift their understanding of the dynamics of their family. Given that they tend to be egocentric, unsure of the limits of their own seemingly powerful wishes and still reluctant to find fault with their parents, they may, in the process of forming their own conclusions about the cause of the divorce, assume that they played a central role in alienating their father from the family.

It is important to recognize the children's confusion and make attempts to alleviate it. A failure to take it into account may have consequences for the child's confidence in his own perceptions of relationships and his understanding of his parents' behavior. For one, this could fuel a fear of further unexpected crises.

Sadness

Intense sadness at the time of the separation is a reaction described by all researchers and clinicians dealing with children of divorce. In 1980, Wallerstein and Kelly described a long lasting somberness as well. Both the acute pain occurring in the aftermath of the separation and the chronic lower intensity sadness which lingers for a long period of time were documented again in this study. As was made clear in Wallerstein and Kelly's most recent work, the lessening or disappearance of the severe pain associated with the early phases of the divorce process was shown not to mean that the child had become happy or even content about the divorce.

Depression

As has already been stressed, the data collected for this study did not allow for systematic clinical diagnosis. Furthermore, while Wallerstein and Kelly indicated the percentage of their total child sample who appeared pathologically depressed at the time of their follow up interviews and explained that latency-age and preadolescent children made up a high proportion of this disturbed group, the exact percentage of this age group affected was not indicated. Therefore, a comparison between the two studies can only be tentative in this regard. An impressionistic appraisal of the present sample however, suggests that differences from Wallerstein and Kelly's sample do exist. While the older children as a group seemed to find thoughts of the divorce more overwhelmingly stressful, the only psychologically disorganized children were at the younger end of the age range. The parents of the two children concerned revealed that psychological problems had preceded the divorce and that therapy had been sought years earlier. With regard to depression which seemed to result from the divorce in reportedly well-adjusted children, the older boys in the sample seemed especially sensitive, as Wallerstein and Kelly also discovered. Of the six children observed to be unusually tense during the interview (to the point where the interviewer concluded that they were dealing with actively felt severe pain), all were boys aged ten through twelve and one-half years. Seven children were seen as especially sad, that is, they were either crying openly or fighting back tears for much of the interview. This latter group consisted of two girls and five boys. In each case, the boys were far more uncomfortable with their upset and/or lack of control over it than the girls. Most apparent in all of these children's interviews was an intense longing for their father even though regular contact was maintained in some cases. Additionally, the children revealed that they experienced a sharp lowering of self-esteem as seen for example, in their extreme discomfort with anyone learning about the divorce. Yet, despite the fact that intense unhappiness was communicated by these children, the sense gained during the brief contact with them and their families was that their depression could only rarely be called severe or pathological. Moreover, these apparently depressed children only comprised one-fourth of the child sample for this research. This suggests that Wallerstein and Kelly were investigating a divorced population skewed towards problematic adjustment. However, the troubled group of youngsters participating in this research do suggest that a vulnerability to postdivorce psychological difficulty does exist for the boys in this age group. The tenacity of the children's sadness, their common inability to express or eradicate their pain, their feelings of low self-worth, and the strength of their feelings of loss involving their father, could be exacerbated to clinical proportions in troubled circumstances (e.g., intense continuing parental hostility). In other words, the differences between the current findings and those of Wallerstein and Kelly (1980) appear to be more of degree than of truly contradictory observations.

Missing Dad

As was the case for sadness, the central role of the children's missing their father was recognized in all previous literature. The reason for the apparent greater importance to the latency-age boys of the daily presence of their father, at least in the period immediately following the divorce, was not explicit in previous research or the present child interviews. The boys' emphasis on their shared male status in their explanations of why they missed their fathers suggests that the boys feel the loss of an identification model. Intermittent contact with the fathers was obviously not satisfactory in this regard. It is also possible that the unavoidable disappointments with their fathers lead to a growing unconscious disenchantment with them that altogether threatens positive identification. The child defensively develops an idealized view of his father and longs for him to return so he can regain the remembered relationship.

Missing the Parental Couple

A major gap in the literature to date is the failure of authors to recognize that missing the mother during visits with the father and missing the parents as a couple is almost as central in the children's divorce experience as missing the father. Only Toomin (1974) touched on this issue in her description of how the child loses the mother-father-child relationship. Because this reaction was never addressed by the interviewer, the children were required to volunteer this information on their own. Even so, about one-third of the sample described this reaction. Those who did stressed its importance to their well being as much as they did missing their father.

Loneliness

In the children's discussion of their loneliness, Toomin's (1974) unique theoretical insights are again given empirical support. Unlike Wallerstein and Kelly and other writers who connected loneliness in this age group solely to the children's longing for their father, Toomin realized the significance of losing both the predivorce father and the predivorce mother. Over half of the children in this sample specifically stated that they were lonely because they received less attention from both parents. Almost the complete child sample (62 of the 66 children interviewed) related that they had felt lonely. Loneliness was also shown to persist through, and in fact, continue to exist because of, the circumstances of postdivorce life. Other than Wallerstein and Kelly's report in 1980 on depression and anger, previous literature provides no sense of which reactions remain active following the divorce and which are only short-lived.

Hope of Reconciliation

The holding onto the hope that their parents would reconcile is one of the reactions where it is believed that Wallerstein and Kelly (1976; Kelly and Wallerstein, 1976) misread the older latency group. While Wallerstein and Kelly reported that fantasies of parental reconciliation were common for younger latency-age children, they did not discuss this reaction when talking about the older children. Yet 56 of the 66 children participating in this study revealed that they had, at least at one point, dreamt about their parents getting back together. Of equal importance is the finding that children hold onto this hope far longer than anyone has anticipated. In 30 cases, it was clear that the children still were wishing a reconciliation would take place. Older and younger latency-age children were about equally represented in this group. Only 13 of the 56 children demonstrated that they now truly accepted the permanence of the divorce.

Anger

Wallerstein and Kelly (1976; Kelly and Wallerstein, 1976) differentiated between the way older and younger latency-age children handled anger. They stated that the younger group was highly defended against expressing anger particularly toward the father. The older group's anger was described as conscious, intense and object-directed. There was a tendency for the older children in this sample to be more direct and open in revealing their anger as well but the children in general were reluctant to discuss how angry they were. Almost two-thirds of the current child sample needed to be questioned before admitting that they had been angry. Several children continued to deny their anger at this point and only admitted it when the issue was addressed indirectly. Furthermore, 18 children (i.e., approximately 27 percent), despite their openness with the interviewer, claimed to have never shown their parents how angry they were about the divorce. (The mothers largely confirmed the children's assertion.) With regard to the object of this anger, it was common for both the older and younger children interviewed for this study to be especially defended against the anger they felt towards their father.

Fears and Concerns

Fear has been discussed by various mental health professionals as a reaction to parental divorce but the findings of this study indicate that it has never been fully examined. Most commonly mentioned is the child's fear that his mother will leave, too. The reports of the children reveal that this fear is not as intense or as frequently experienced as a fear of never seeing the father again. Only slightly more than one-third of the sample agreed that they were concerned about their mother leaving and all but three of these children did not raise the subject until questioned directly. In contrast, a majority of the sample described their fear of totally losing their father and demonstrated that this anxiety strongly compounded their pain upon his departure from the household. Nagging doubts about the permanence of the father's love for them appear to remain for a long time. Another spontaneously mentioned fear which has received almost no attention in the divorce literature is the fear that the parents will get severely hurt or killed. Although Wallerstein and Kelly (1980) stated that by the time of the first follow up, crisis-evoked responses such as fear had lessened or disappeared altogether, most of the 34 children in this study who showed an intense concern about their parents' vulnerability continued to have this worry at the present time. It seems likely that the number of children who expressed this ongoing fear would be even higher if a direct inquiry had been made.

The Pressures of Having Divorced Parents

According to the children participating in this study, the more mature roles assigned to them since the parental separation were burdensome at times but did not typically feel overwhelming or pathological. In another context however, some children revealed how upset they became when their mother shared the intimate details of the marriage problems with them. The ways in which a mother's dependence on her children could reach pathological proportions was thus evident but more often the strength of the children in helping their mother through a crisis was apparent. This study thus supports Wallerstein and Kelly's 1976 finding that older children often become emotional supports and practical helpers for their parents. The possible problems outlined by Weiss (1979) were only rarely seen.

Positive Reactions

Positive reactions were not found to predominate in the current sample's experience. Wallerstein and Kelly (1980) stated that girls were more likely to view divorce as an improvement over the family situation prior to the separation. This viewpoint was held by two girls in this study but no others. Wallerstein and Kelly's observation that the divorce was typically accepted but not considered to be a good idea, more closely approximates the current findings but the discovery that almost half of the children still held the hope that their parents would reconcile, suggests that even this conclusion is overstated.

Mothers' Views of Their Children's Reactions

Mothers have likely been used as a source of information on their children's divorce experience more often than has been recorded. Three researchers however, have specified that their reports of the children's reactions were based just on contact with the parents. Goode (1956) devoted a chapter of his book to the mothers' views of their children although he showed no interest in the specific reactions which a divorce evokes. Weiss (1975), in the section of his book concerning the children, mainly summarized other researchers' findings but also briefly gave the parents' view of what their children were feeling. In so doing, he provided a sense of the possible range of some of the major reactions. As one aspect of a broader study, Fulton (1979) focused on mothers' and fathers' assessment of their children's adjustment following divorce. She gathered information from 560 divorced parents, representative of the urban counties in Minnesota from which the sample was drawn. Results are based on the analyses of parental responses to a symptom checklist and to a question concerning the overall impact of divorce on the children.

Both Goode and Weiss presented the mothers' reports with the sole purpose of providing some details on the children's reactions to balance their primary interest in the mothers' experience. However, they seemed to lose sight of the fact that they were only getting one facet of the situation and often presented the material as an accurate account of the children's feelings. Their failure to obtain the children's views of the same time period gave them no reason to question the validity of their findings.

Fulton's primary interest was examining the parents' view of the overall impact of divorce and the factors affecting the parents' perceptions. She found that 48 percent of the mothers believed that the divorce had a negative effect on their children. No detail on the nature of the negative change was provided but Fulton's explanation of the variables which were significantly associated with the mothers' assessment echoes the views related earlier in this paper. As was true for the present sample, the mothers in the Minnesota study saw their own role as central to the child's adjustment while they downplayed the importance of the father-child relationship. In general, Fulton learned that a mother was more likely to describe the children as negatively affected by the divorce if she was greatly distressed by it and positively affected if she was relieved to leave a marriage filled with frequent and/or violent arguments.

Because of the nature of Fulton's and Goode's report, the following section of this chapter is largely a comparison with the findings of Weiss. Weiss's work however, is a short summary so that depth, in most instances, is lacking.

Surprise and Confusion

Weiss talked of children's distress and anxiety upon learning of the impending divorce but did not mention surprise or confusion. Although mothers reported these reactions far less frequently than did the children, over one-third of the mothers in this study did observe that their children were surprised and confused.

Sadness

In terms of the numbers of women who agreed that their children felt sad and the tendency of many mothers to view their children's recovery from the pain associated with the divorce as rapid, Weiss's report was similar to the present study. Weiss's parents seemed to underestimate the duration of their children's unhappiness considerably more frequently than the women in the present study but given that he does not provide any numbers, an exact comparison is not possible.

Hope of Reconciliation

The mothers described by Weiss and the mothers participating in this study considered a hope of reconciliation to be one of the most common reactions to divorce. Their descriptions of how the children communicated their wish and sometimes tried to make it happen, were also similar. The close parallel between the two studies, with regard to an elaboration of this reaction, is likely due to the fact that the children's hopes for their parents getting back together are usually obvious even with little sensitivity on the parents' part. As indicated earlier, no time frame for this reaction is provided by Weiss.

Anger

In describing the children's anger at their parents, Weiss touched upon many of the same points as were elucidated in the current study. Anger was seen as a common reaction in both studies. It was observed to be most often directed at the one parent who was held responsible for the divorce. Furthermore, both direct and indirect methods of expressing anger were discussed by the two groups of mothers. However, Weiss's assertion that children commonly demonstrated their anger at their father by refusing to see him was not given support. Additionally, Weiss did not discuss the various parental behaviors postdivorce which triggered the children's resentment.

Goode (1956) stated that 25 percent of the children observed by the mothers in his study, were described as "harder to handle" after returning home from visits with their father. Visits were also mentioned as a cause for irritable or aggressive behavior in a minority of cases by the mothers in the current sample.

Fears and Concerns

The mothers, upon whom Weiss based his analysis, believed that their children's concerns focused on their own situation. For example, they worried about where they would live, when they would see their father, or who would take care of them in the event that their mother became unavailable. These worries were revealed through questions when the news of the divorce was shared with the children and were considered to be soon eliminated by the parents' answers. Additionally, "younger" children were seen as afraid that they were responsible for the separation; "older" children were viewed as uneasy about the future. Although Weiss did not imply that all children were observed to have experienced all the fears mentioned, he did write as if the general topic of fear of what would happen to them was raised by all the mothers involved in the study. Either Weiss is generalizing from a few cases or the mothers with whom he had contact were far more sensitive on this issue than the mothers participating in this study. The mothers in this sample did not stress the significance of fear as a reaction to divorce. In fact they needed to be directly questioned for most of their opinions in this area. Less than half of the mothers, sometimes considerably less, described each type of anxiety. As was true for Weiss's study, when fear was discussed, mention was made of the children's initial questions. Neither Weiss nor the mothers in the current study talked of fear as an ongoing feeling.

Positive Reactions

Weiss mentioned the possibility that relief might occur in a few stressful situations. The mothers in this study recognized that relief was not a major reaction but referred to it more frequently. Additionally, slightly less than one-fourth of the sample discussed their view that the divorce resulted in an improvement in the children's self-esteem and more generally relaxed functioning. This finding is similar to Fulton's report (1979) that approximately 20 percent of the mothers believed that, overall, their children's adjustment improved following the divorce.

8

How the Reports of Mother and Child
Fit Together

It was seen earlier how the mothers and children, when viewed as a total group, described each other's reactions. This initial step toward analyzing the interrelationship of individual family members' reactions to the divorce process is furthered in the current chapter. The focus of study now shifts to the specific ways in which the reports of the mother and the children in each family fit together.

Where Mothers See Differences between Their Own Reactions to the Divorce Process and Those of Their Children

When the areas in which the mothers perceived differences between their own and their children's reactions are examined the conclusions are surprising. The surprise comes however, not from which reactions are seen to differentiate the mother's divorce experience from her child's but how infrequently most reactions are mentioned. The most commonly cited differences are that the children wanted a parental reconciliation whereas the mother (after some possible early consideration) did not, and that the children missed their father whereas the mother did not or did so only rarely. Yet, only the first of these differences accounts for more than half the child sample; the latter applies to slightly less than half. Other important differences are mentioned less often, usually by fewer than one third of the mothers.

    The observation that the mother's reactions to the divorce differs in the above two ways indicated that in approximately half of the cases, the women interviewed recognized that their children's orientation to the parental separation is fundamentally different from their own. That is, they understood that an outcome of divorce for the typical separating couple is a withdrawal of investment in the relationship and the ex-spouse while the child remains committed to the parents as a couple and to a continuing relationship with his father. However, this difference is not considered to be applicable for the remaining portion of the child sample. Furthermore, with regard to the other major reactions to divorce, a large majority of mothers see their experience as quite similar to their children's.

Although it is not known if this failure to differentiate their own reaction to a situation from that of their children is unique to the divorce experience, these mothers' perceptions are indicative of a family dynamic in which generational boundaries are disregarded. Conflict is avoided by the assumption that the entire family responds similarly.

While, as mentioned in chapter 3 where the considerable range of divorce experiences was discussed, certain circumstances such as the father unilaterally initiating the divorce can apparently cause the reactions of mother and child to be more clearly parallel, the high number of women who assumed few differences existed between their own and their children's reactions reflects, in large part, a lack of insight in several families. This failure to perceive accurately the children's reactions is confirmed by an examination of those reactions which the child insisted he felt but which the mother believed were not experienced. Although the number of mothers who stated that their children wanted a reconciliation closely matches the number of children who said they hoped for this (i.e., only five children's feelings were overlooked), this accuracy is not present to the same extent for children missing their father. In nine cases, the mother totally missed the fact that her son or daughter missed his/her father a great deal. In 14 more cases, the mother realized that the child had missed the father somewhat but did not grasp the extent of the child's feelings of loss or the intensity of the child's longing. (Since no quantified measure of the degree to which a child misses his father was attempted, this latter situation was only tallied when the discrepancy between the mother's and child's report was large and very obvious.)

This same trend is repeated when other areas of differences in reactions, cited by the mothers, are studied. Approximately one-third of the children were seen to have fears triggered by the divorce situation but these fears were believed to be different from the ones their mother experienced. The children's reports reveal that this proportion is as low as it is because the mothers often failed to recognize that their children were afraid at all. A review of the child interviews demonstrated that the mothers of 21 children (almost one-third of the sample) totally missed observing their children's fears. In eight of these cases the children were shown to be extremely afraid of numerous aspects of their new situation (e.g., not seeing their father again, their parents getting killed, running out of money, etc.).

At times, the sort of underestimation of the impact of divorce on their children which led mothers to *miss* differences between their children's reactions and their own, produced the opposite result. With regard to a few reactions, mothers related that their feelings differed from their children's when, in fact, no difference existed or the difference was of a nature other than the mother suspected. Two of the more frequently cited instances of this type of error involved anger and fear. More than one-third of the children were described as having no anger towards their father or feeling only a little bit angry while their mother felt very angry. As is evident from the child interviews, the mother failed to notice her child's anger at his father in 18 cases. The mother assumed that only she felt anything negative towards her ex-husband when this was indeed, not true. Similarly, with regard to over one-fourth of the child sample, the mothers stated that they had felt very afraid of the unknown future whereas their children were relaxed about it or far less afraid. It was just shown that mothers of 21 children did not see the fear their children experienced because of the divorce. Moreover, in 23 additional cases, the mother did not see all of her child's fears and, in six more, she was not able to delineate any of the child's fears despite her sense that he had been afraid.

Although, as has been shown, a large percentage of the women participating in this study failed to perceive accurately several differences between their own reactions and those of their children, the mothers are certainly not mistaken in all their observations. Some differences in reactions stem from the dissimilar roles the various family members play in the divorce decision (e.g., the mother may take an active part in planning the separation). Hence, seven mothers, referring to 12 children, talked of the emotional turmoil and tension they experienced prior to the decision to separate which was absent for the children. Relatedly, with regard to 20 children (almost one-third of the sample), the mothers felt relieved when the separation finally occurred while the children did not. Other differences, cited by the mothers result from the specific changes which occurred in their daily lives. Most commonly, a mother talked of feeling overwhelmed by all her responsibilities while her children became more demanding or simply did not share this feeling. (This was seen as true for 20 mother-child pairs.) Another difference related to the mother's need to cope with her new position as a single woman, that is, she doubted her attractiveness to men while no parallel reaction existed for the children. This was mentioned as applying to 19 mother-child pairs. Finally, the children are expected to maintain a relationship with both parents while the husband-wife relationship is sharply curtailed. In 20 cases the mother pointed out that the children felt torn between their parents, remaining loyal to both, while the mother just felt negatively about her ex-husband.

The remaining differences mentioned by the mothers are listed in table 2. This list includes several differences which occurred more frequently than the mothers realized.

Table 2. Differences in Reactions Described by the Mothers

	Number of Mother-Child Pairs
Children surprised by news of divorce, not mother	17
Children confused, not mother	8
Mother needing to get out—work and/or socialize, child wanted her home, felt unloved or angry when she went out	12
Mother felt isolated from former friends, not children	18
Mother guilty, not children	14
Mother very lonely or lonely at times, children not lonely or much less so	12
Mother felt rejected by the father, not true for the child	7
Mother self-absorbed, children able to be supportive of her	7
Mother fairly calm about the future, children nervous at first	5
Mother saw her life as changing radically, children's remaining very much the same	5
Children felt somewhat rejected by their father, mother took part in decision	6
Child angry about divorce, mother wanted it	10
Mother angry at the father, children just angry at the mother (at least for a time)	9
Children angry at both parents, mother angry at father	17

Table 2 (continued)

Mother felt positive about divorce, believing life had improved, children did not feel this way	5
During time after separation life was more enjoyable for the mother, child felt insecure and upset	5
Mother's negative feelings largely resolved by the time of the final separation, children upset	11
Mother's pain more intense although both upset	8
Mother felt intensely upset for a long time, children recovered quickly	11

Where Children See Differences in Reactions

As was the case for the mothers, children most frequently pointed out those differences in reactions which reflected their opposing orientations to the parents' marital relationship (i.e., as the mothers resolved to withdraw investment from their relationship with their husband, the children longed for their father to return home). The children however, went even further in emphasizing how much they wished the divorce had not occurred. In addition to most commonly mentioning that they missed their father while their mother did not, and that they wanted a parental reconciliation while their mother did not, the children also described how their mother had a role in the divorce decision even if it saddened her while they did not want the divorce at all. The first two differences were referred to by approximately half of the children; the latter by one-third of the child sample. Mothers it seems, are not generally attuned to how adamantly against the divorce their children remain and consequently how much this issue differentiates the child's divorce experience from the mother's.

Several other differences between their own reactions and those of their mother are mentioned more often in the child interviews than they were by the mothers. Between one-third and one-half of the child sample talked about how they were surprised while their mother was not, how they were uncomfortable/ashamed about the divorce while their mother was not, and how both they and their mother had fears related to the divorce but ones of a different nature. All of these alleged differences appear to be accurate assessments of the varying reactions which divorce triggers for mothers and children. However, fear is even more widespread for mothers than their children realized. Six children erroneously contended that they were scared while their mother was not or much less so. A closer examination of the differences in fears noted by the children also reveals that children, even when they recognized that their mother was afraid to some extent, missed out on the number of different things which caused her to be afraid. Typically, children saw themselves as worried about many aspects of their future and their continuing relationship with their parents, while they viewed their mother as chiefly worried about having enough money or about the children's reactions. In total, 17 children failed to see all of their mother's fears.

The one area in which children commonly viewed a difference to have existed between their own reaction and their mother's which often resulted from a misperception on the part of the children, concerns their belief that their mother quickly recovered from any pain associated with the divorce. Specifically, just under one-third of the children contended that they had more to adjust to in the divorce situation than their mother or that their mother simply had an easier time adjusting to the separation. Additionally, between one-fourth and one-third of the children stated that their mother felt good when the divorce was over while they were still upset.

Although it is difficult to ascertain if the children did indeed find it more difficult than their mother to adjust to this change in their life, it is clear from the mothers' reports that the children do not always perceive the extent of the mother's pain. Thirteen children severely underestimated the intensity of their mother's depression. Moreover, 10 children missed the fact that choosing to initiate the divorce was a very difficult decision for their mother or that she was very unhappy or tense prior to making the decision. They did not realize that although their mother may have appeared to have resolved her feelings about the divorce more quickly than the children, her unhappiness in fact, preceded the children's. Finally, 25 children did not observe that their mother felt unlovable or worthless following the separation. That is, even if unlike the child she adjusted rather easily to living without the father, she still had painful feelings resulting from the breakdown of the marriage.

Table 3 lists the remaining differences cited by the children and the frequency with which they were mentioned. All of the differences were noticed by less than one-fourth of the child sample. At times, the small number of children to describe a specific difference represents a failure of the group as a whole to observe differences where they in reality existed (e.g., mother feels guilty, not the child). These misperceptions will become apparent in the section of this chapter focusing on the reactions of mothers which children missed.

Table 3. Differences in Reactions Described by the Children

	Number of Mother-Child Pairs
Mother angry at father, not child or child much less so	12
Child angry at both parents as did not want a divorce, mother angry at father about a lot of things	15
Child concerned about father, mother angry at him	6
Child angry at mother for divorce, mother wanting it	8
Mother feels guilty, not child	8
Mother feels exceedingly negative about father, child loves him	7
Mother needing to adjust to all her responsibilities, no similar change for child	5
Mother wanting to go out, child feels unloved or afraid when she does, wants her to stay home	5
Child lonely, not mother	5
Mother has mixed feelings about divorce, child just sad	7
Mother had a harder time adjusting than child, more depressed than child	5
Some things improved for mother, she felt positively about divorce, not child	7

The Impact of Differences in Reactions on the Mother/Child Relationship and Family Functioning

All the differences in reactions which have been discussed, whether or not they reflect a correct perception of the other family member's feelings, represent areas in which mothers and/or children believe their response to the divorce to be unique. At times, this thought can be comforting to the mother, particularly when she feels the children are having an easier time than she adjusting to the divorce. Thus, she is relieved if while her negative feelings continue unabated, the children's seem to be of brief duration and/or little intensity. Especially in families where the mother was the primary instigator of the divorce, such a view eases her guilt for creating a situation which might cause her children pain.

> *They would say "I hate daddy for doing that to you" and that was horrible because I never wanted them to hate him. That was brief, that was at that time and now everything is just fine. That's what's so beautiful about children. They forgive and forget so easily.*

More typically, differences in reactions largely cause the individual to feel more isolated in his attempts to cope with the divorce. The children interviewed commonly asserted that they felt bad long after everyone else returned to life as usual. They often kept this view to themselves, thus increasing their sense of aloneness.

> C: *Well when I felt sad about it my mom kind of felt a little glad.*
> I: *What happened then?*
> C: *Then I didn't talk to her that much because I was mad.... I really don't talk about it that much and I don't say anything because it just makes me sorry to talk about it.*

Attempts at raising the issue with their mother however, frequently met with unsatisfactory results. Several children reported that their mother clearly indicated her wish to change the topic.

> *...but she really didn't want to talk about it and stuff.... She just starts talking to the person, like interrupting me or something.*

The same impact is apparent with regard to the children wanting a reconciliation and missing their father. Although the latter is often evident to the mothers in the child's questions concerning arrangements for the next visit, these issues are typically not otherwise discussed except in the immediate aftermath of the separation. Children report that airing their feelings only seems to stress their mother so that they learn at least outwardly, to accept the changes in their family.

Hetherington (1977) commented that divorced parents tend to communicate poorly with their children and that both parents and children were less affectionate than individuals from families in which the parents remained married. Although it is not universally evident, this conclusion seems to be supported by the assertions of many of the children in this study and appears to result from a perceived difference in feelings about the divorce. A coping style consisting of trying to ignore any issues which might cause upset, present in many of these families, adds to the communication deadlock.

For mothers, the period during which they feel their experience differs most vastly from the children and consequently when they feel most distant from them is often the time prior to the separation. During this period many women reported that they were extremely tense and unhappy both because of the difficulty they were having relating to their husband and because of the gravity of arriving at a decision to initiate a divorce. The children were rarely seen as sharing these feelings and in fact, were commonly regarded as oblivious to the mother's emotional turmoil.

> *I went through feelings that it would be terribly selfish but I'm so terribly unhappy that I knew something had to happen. I knew that I would get no support from family if I did decide to divorce. The biggest problem was that I was afraid that it would affect my kids greatly; that's what everybody reacts to when they think about someone getting divorced. They say "oh those poor kids." You don't identify with the pain the mother's going through or the father's going through or the reason for it.... The toughest thing for me was trying to make the decision.... When my husband left and I told the children, Sam just couldn't believe it, I mean it was like what was wrong. He didn't know. I didn't tell him.... My kids didn't tell me that they hated me or anything like that but they were very angry that they can't go on living as a foursome even if you are miserable. Sam said "I don't care whether you want to live with dad or not but I want a family" and all I could say is I can't do that for you.*

Certain differences in reactions are more likely than others to create stress in the mother-child relationship. Differences in whether anger is experienced or not as well as differences regarding the object of this anger are ones that especially serve to isolate a mother from her children. Most mothers related that they are concerned about their children and know that any expression of anger on their part towards their ex-husband upsets the children. Their anger is something which they feel must remain hidden. When it does emerge they often react by feeling guilty for making the children uncomfortable and/or for interfering with the continuation of a positive father-child relationship.

> *Yes, especially when he would do something that would set it off. It would be hard not to just yell up and down, and I know I shouldn't have done it and a couple of times I did bad mouth him and I felt, I strongly feel that they shouldn't be brought into it because they are kind of more or less innocent bystanders. It's between the two adults; it's not between the children and then they feel guilty for loving the other one and I think it makes it worse for them too.*

There is at times however, a wish that the children would share their wrath and a tension produced because the children's feelings appear so blatantly positive. Mothers may occasionally come to resent their children for feeling so differently and attempt to convince them of their views.

> *Jim does not question his father on whatever he tells him. What he says is everything that's okay, and that's right if his father says it to him. . . . It's to the point now that I really, he's* [her ex-husband] *really beginning to get on my nerves a lot lately and I'm to the point where I really don't care if I make an excuse for him or not. Let the kids, you know, tell it the way it is and I'm getting sick of making excuses for him and making him always out to be, like that he is the good guy. They see very little of him and you know they have him up on a pedestal like and then when he calls and says that he is not picking them up or he does this and he does that.*

The ability to empathize with the children's reactions and be supportive of their feelings is made especially difficult when the mother, who has a great deal of anger for her husband, believes that he is spared anger which he deserves, while she is the target of considerable animosity.

The children, in turn, are upset and often angered by the mother's expression of anger, especially when this continues after the divorce decree has been granted and the source of the mother's anger is not understood.

> I: Do you think that a boy would be angry at his mom about the divorce?
> C: *Maybe after a whole month he gets like thinking really hard, and like he's just writing letters, if he's writing letters and asks his mom*

"How come you won't talk to Dad?"... Yeah, like stuff when Dad wrote notes to her sometimes, she'd tear it up and that makes you think about your dad.

Knowledge of their mother's hostility regarding their father also may lead to the children avoiding any mention of him and in so doing, keeping a great deal of their thoughts to themselves.

I: What do you do when she's angry at Dad?
C: *Help her not think about Dad, not mention Dad.*

Another difference in reactions which serves to create a rift in the postdivorce family is the mother needing to get out of the house and involve herself in some aspect of starting a new life (e.g., her job or her social life) while the children want to keep her home. In order for the mother to meet her own needs she thus believes that she must cause the children additional pain. If her view of the children's feelings is that they feel unloved or lonely, her desire to leave them causes her to feel that she is in an untenable position and guilty whenever she chooses to satisfy her own wishes. On the other hand, if she largely regards the children as being overly possessive of her and selfish, guilt often becomes replaced with resentment.

There were times when I just didn't know how to cope with it. I didn't know what to do because I tried everything. I tried being stern with him, I tried to be sympathetic with him, and I just felt that nothing was working. I think you get to the point that you don't think you can cope with it.... It would make me feel guilty but then I knew that I could not let him control my life. Because I knew that kids will try to control you if they can.

Finally, the mother's acceptance of at least partial responsibility for the divorce contrasted with the totally passive role of the children, and the guilty feelings which ensue, appear to impact greatly on the manner in which a family functions postdivorce. Compounded by other reactions such as her feeling overwhelmed, the mother's guilt often leads to inconsistency in discipline. Typically the mother alternates between attempting to make up for the loss of their father by being extremely lenient in disciplining the children and then compensates for this attitude by becoming rigid in her demands.

I'm trying to be more strict with him and not let him rule me instead of, you know, whatever they want to do. I tend to be too easygoing with them because I'm going all day long and then I get home at night. You know, I let them do a lot of things and get away with a lot of things that I shouldn't

*_et away with because I feel more or less kind of guilty of being
from them so much than I already am, you know, all day long and
ometimes.

The Impact of Sex, Sibling Order and Visitation Arrangement on Where Differences in Reactions Are Seen

In evaluating the importance of the sex of the child, his/her position in the sibling pair, and the frequency of father visitation, for affecting where a mother or child observes differences in their reactions, the number of interviewees mentioning any one difference must be taken into account. Because for the most part the numbers are very small, several instances exist where an observable trend is present but where a statistically significant impact of a particular variable is not achieved. It is quite possible that in a larger sample the findings would be more conclusive. On the other hand, in situations where a significant effect is demonstrated, this result is achieved despite the small number of individuals concerned and reflects the fact that an extremely high proportion of the sample was affected by the variable studied. These statistically significant findings therefore reveal a great deal about families' reactions to divorce. Significance was tested in all instances by the chi square test of independence.

With regard to the two most frequently cited differences between the reactions of a mother and her children, that is, those concerning the wish for a parental reconciliation (child wants it, mother does not) and missing the father (child does, mother does not at all or only rarely), the sex of the child was not found to influence either the mothers' or the children's views. Likewise sibling order and the frequency of visitation were shown to have no impact on the mothers' thinking about either of these differences or the children's on missing their father. However, these last two variables did seem to be important determinants of whether children discussed the issue of their wanting a reconciliation while their mother did not.

Older children were more likely than their younger sibling to point out that they had wanted their parents to reconcile whereas their mother did not share this wish. Although the effect of sibling position is not statistically significant ($.20 > p > .10$), the percentage of older children is considerably different than it is in the overall sample. Older children commented that they hoped their parents would get back together in contrast to their mother's wishes in 21 cases (58.3 percent of older children) as compared to 12 (40 percent of younger children) for their younger sibling. This difference appears to stem from two sources. First, the younger child in a family seems to be less aware in general of differences between their own reactions and those of their mother due both to their overall younger age and their more babied position in the family. Second, older children appear to be more opposed to the divorce and to maintain their objections for a longer period.

Children who frequently visit with their father also comment more often that they wish for a reconciliation whereas their mother does not, although again the impact only approaches significance ($.20 > p > .10$). As above however, the greater percentage of children with frequent visitation is impressive. In the child sample as a whole, 57.6 percent of the children had regular visitation; of the 33 children who noted this difference 66.7 percent had regular visitation. It seems that children with regular visitation find the alternative of a reconciliation more appealing because they have a more involved relationship with their father and also because they see their parents in positive contact more frequently. As observed previously, parents in families with regular visitation appear to feel less hostility towards each other. It is also likely that the opportunity to see his parents together on a regular basis fuels the child's reconciliation fantasies. Both explanations suggest that perceived differences between mothers and children, with regard to their attitude toward reconciliation, are primarily dependent on the strength of the child's feelings.

For the purposes of this analysis and all others in this chapter regarding the influence of visitation arrangements, frequent visitation is defined as those situations in which the father gets together with his children at least once every other week on a regular basis. Infrequent visitation therefore refers to the situation in the remaining families. In all cases, fathers in this sample who saw their children less frequently than once every other week were also irregular and unpredictable in their pattern of contacting the children (i.e., time between visits ranges considerably).

Although the mothers' and children's perceptions of differences regarding the hope for a parental reconciliation and missing the father were shown to be formulated independently of considerations concerning the sex of the child in question, this conclusion is not true for differences related to anger. No significant difference is shown between the sexes, likely because of the small number of children involved, when the mother's belief that she was angry at the father while the children were angry at her, is examined. (Whereas the total N for all statistical comparisons in this section is equal to the number of children interviewed, that is 66, this particular difference was pointed out for only nine mother-child pairs.) However, boys are mentioned twice as often in this regard as girls. When the mother's contention that she was angry at the father while her child was angry at both parents is analyzed, the opposite influence is revealed. Daughters are represented here more than twice as often as sons, a difference which is shown to be significant ($p < 0.10$). In keeping with the above findings boys are referred to over twice as frequently when mothers stated that they were angry at the father whereas their child was not angry or only a little angry. The impact of the sex of the child on this last observed difference is highly significant (p $<$ .01).

It has already been described that the mother's belief that her child does not share her anger towards her ex-husband but instead idealizes him is a source of friction in the mother-child relationship. Moreover, it was stated that this friction is exacerbated when the only object of the child's hostility is the mother. The finding that both of these stresses are more common between mothers and their sons is thus very important in understanding the problems a family faces in coping with divorce.

The finding that more stress exists between mothers and sons than mothers and daughters, at least with respect to one aspect of the postdivorce situation, reiterates an observation made by Hetherington (1977, 1978) with preschool children. The present analysis however, presents an interesting contrast to the conclusions of Wallerstein and Kelly (1980). They had observed that boys, in their stronger opposition to the divorce, remained intensely angry and upset when their female counterparts demonstrated progressive adjustment to the divorce. This view, whether or not it is accurate for the current sample, is not one maintained by the mothers interviewed for this study. Although boys are sometimes described as generally rebellious, the women do not notice their sons as more angry about the divorce, at least in terms of feelings towards their father, (Wallerstein and Kelly had not specified to whom the boys directed their anger). Rather, they perceive their sons as loyal to their father and protective of him.

The sex of the child is definitely the important variable in the mother's formulation of her thoughts concerning the differences between her feelings of anger and her children's. However, with regard to the mother feeling angry at her ex-husband while her children feel angry at both parents, a significant visitation effect is also seen. This last difference is mentioned over four times as often in families where a regular visitation schedule has been followed (p $<$ 0.02). Although the mothers interviewed did not explain this finding as follows, it is likely that the child feels more secure in general when close contact is kept with the father and is therefore more comfortable expressing anger toward both parents. Anger, especially towards the father, needs to be suppressed when there is danger of threatening an already tenuous relationship. Mothers simply appear more likely to notice the anger which is evoked by some disliked aspect of the child's visits with his father (e.g., his inviting a girlfriend to share their time together) than the resentment at the father for becoming more extremely inattentive.

Variation in visitation arrangements is the strongest factor affecting children's views about anger. Children with infrequent visitation are represented twice as often as children with frequent visitation (p $<$ 0.10). This finding supports the earlier supposition that is is difficult for a child to express anger when he does not have a steady relationship with his father. All anger is denied in the process of longing for a closer relationship. The results of analysis concerning the difference—mother angry at father, child angry at both parents—provides further evidence for this conclusion. Children who frequently get together with their father relate this difference four times as often as children with infrequent visitation. The probability of this difference occurring by chance is less than .05.

No other differences in reactions observed by mothers show a significant impact of the sex of the child. However an examination of three reported differences suggests that sex may still be a factor influencing the mother's observations. In all three cases the data results exhibit a trend towards the mother seeing her son as having more difficulty adjusting to the divorce than her daughter. That is, the daughter is more often considered to react differently from her mother when a difference connotes that the mother is having a negative reaction and the child is not. Conversely, the son is more often considered to react differently when a difference connotes that the mother is having less of a negative reaction than the child. The first of these differences involved the mother feeling guilty while the child does not. That is mentioned over twice as often referring to girls, a sex difference which approaches significance ($0.20 > p > 0.10$). Likewise, in instances where the mother claims she felt very lonely while her child did not feel lonely at all or much less so, girls are again mentioned two times as frequently. (The number of cases is small and no significant impact is shown.) Yet, when the mother states that the child felt ashamed with friends whereas the mother did not, mother-son pairs are accounted for twice as often as mother-daughter pairs.

Table 4 lists the results of analysis of the impact of sex on the differences cited by mothers. In contrast to the women, the children's explanations of differences between their own divorce experience and that of their mother do not appear to be influenced in any important ways by the sex of the child. Table 5 summarizes these findings.

Overall, the impact of sibling order on the mother's citing of differences between her own reactions and her child's is negligible. This finding supports similar conclusions of Wallerstein and Kelly.

For children, the influence of sibling order is limited but some interesting observations can be made. In addition to the already mentioned effect on the children's view of differences involving parental reconciliation, there is a significant impact of sibling order when the children raise the issue of fear. Of the 30 children who discussed the difference between the fear they experienced and how their mother reacted to her new situation, 20 children were the older child in the family ($p < 0.10$). The older children thus regard themselves as

Table 4.   Interrelation of Sex of the Child and the Areas in Which
Mothers Noted Differences in Reactions

Differences in Reactions	Chi Square*	Level of Significance
Mother guilty, not children	2.42	.20 > p > .10
Mother very lonely, children not or much less so	1.10	N.S.
Child ashamed with friends, not mother	1.62	N.S.
Mother angry at father, children angry at mother	1.62	N.S.
Mother angry at father, child angry at both parents	2.83	p < .10
Mother angry at father, not children and children only a little	8.52	p < .01
Mother angry at father, children only a little	7.12	p < .01

(All other differences were not analyzed statistically as the difference between the sexes was obviously negligible.)

*Degrees of freedom for all analysis here and in subsequent sections of this chapter is 1.

frightened more frequently whether or not they believe their mother was afraid. The difference between the siblings' views diverges most when the child describes herself as scared while the mother has no fears or is only minimally afraid. The direction of these differences at first seems contrary to logic if one assumes that the older child can understand the reality of the situation better and that many fears are largely irrational. What seems likely is that as older children are considered by their mothers to be more grown-up and are given greater responsibility, they are thrust into an independence and certain family roles (e.g., caretaker for their younger sibling) for which they are not entirely ready. The life of the younger child changes less as he continues to be more babied.

It is important to note that older and younger here do not refer to the age of the child but the position of the child in the sibling relationship. While it is true that the average age for the older sibling is indeed higher, many of the

Table 5.   Interrelation of Sex of the Child and the Areas in Which
Children Noted Differences in Reactions

Differences in Reactions	Chi Square	Level of Significance
Mother angry at father, child not and only a little	2.28	.20 > p > .10
Child angry at both parents, mother angry at father	1.45	N.S.
Mother had a harder time adjusting, more depressed than child	1.58	N.S.
Child has more to adjust to, mother has an easier time of it	1.28	N.S.
Mother played a role in the divorce decision, choosing it even if sad, child altogether did not want it	1.49	N.S.
Mother feels good when it's over, not child	1.25	N.S.
Child scared, mother not scared at all or much less so (N = 6; all girls)	3.96	p < .05
Child scared as well as mother but different fears are noted (N = 24; 15 boys, 9 girls)	3.65	p < .10

"younger" children in the sample are older than many of the "older" siblings and vice versa. Table 6 details the effect of sibling position.

The impact of sibling order on the children's thinking, while not extensive, does suggest that this factor warrants some attention. This is the first study to find that sibling order influences a family's responses to divorce and the only study besides that of Wallerstein and Kelly to address the issue at all.

The nature of the visitation arrangement between her children and her ex-husband clearly affects the mother's responses in a couple of areas. First,

Table 6.   Interrelation of Sibling Position and the Areas in Which
Children Noted Differences in Reactions

Differences in Reactions	Chi Square	Level of Significance
Mother angry at father, not child	2.86	p < .10
Child wanted reconciliation, not mother	2.2	.20 > p > .10
Child has more to adjust to, mother has an easier time of it	.67	N.S.
Mother had role in divorce decision, choosing it even if it made her sad, child altogether did not want it	1.1	N.S.
Child scared, mother not or much less so	2.2	.20 > p > .10
Combined differences: Child scared, mother not or much less so, and Child scared as well as mother but fears are different	3.26	p < .10

mothers stated that they felt lonely whereas their children did not feel lonely at all or did but only a very little, much more often when a regular visitation routine had been established (p < .05). It appears that seeing her ex-husband frequently accentuates a woman's loneliness. Moreover, since mothers typically connect their children's loneliness to missing their father, frequent visits are seen to abate or eliminate the child's loneliness altogether. It is also likely that, when visitation is regular, a woman believes that her child's life has remained more as it was before the divorce, especially in contrast to her own, so that there is less of a reaction in general to the divorce process.

Second, instances of a woman pointing out that her child only experienced a minor upset of brief duration while she was intensely upset for a long period, are found overwhelmingly in families where visitation is irregular (p < .02 with Yates's correction). It might have been predicted that a mother would view her children as more upset in these situations but of the 11 mother-child pairs mentioned, nine children saw their father infrequently. This accounts for approximately one-third of all the children who visited with their father on an irregular basis. It seems that according to their mothers, children are capable of recovering quickly from any pain triggered by the divorce when they have no contact with their father or perhaps even adjusting more easily because they see him so rarely. In terms of the mother's greater upset, it appears that irregular visitation often follows a situation which the mother found particularly upsetting such as her husband becoming involved with a new woman. Furthermore, the father's lack of involvement with the children and lack of assistance to her in raising them intensifies her pain. It appears that mothers view irregular visitation as having a negative affect on their ability to adjust to the divorce compared to their children.

Table 7 addresses the impact of the frequency of visitation on where mothers see differences. One very important effect of the nature of the visitation arrangement on where a child observes differences to exist between his own reactions and his mother's has already been addressed in the previous discussion of differences related to anger. Two other areas of significant impact are also evident. When a child states that his mother had a role in the divorce decision, choosing it even if it made her sad, while the child did not want the divorce at all, he appears to be influenced in his thinking by the fact that he visits frequently with his father. Sixteen children with regular visitation reported this difference whereas only six with irregular visitation did so ($p < .10$). This difference is not dependent on the child's not wanting the divorce as the preference for continuing the parents' marriage is maintained by most children, but rather on the view that the mother was active in procuring the divorce. Regular visitation, which has already been shown to be associated with the mother feeling less frequently hurt or intensely depressed, is also clearly linked in the children's mind with the mother wanting the divorce.

The final area of significant visitation effect involves the various fear reactions. In all cases where children stated that they were scared because of the divorce while their mothers were not or much less so, a regular visitation routine had been established ($p < .10$ with Yates's correction). Conversely, in a majority of cases where the children stated that they were scared as well as their mother, but of different things, no visitation schedule was followed ($p < .05$). It seems that regular visitation does not eliminate the children's fears but does appear to the children to relax their mother. The fears most commonly cited by the children as being experienced by their mother are money worries and concerns about the children's reactions. It seems logical that fathers who visit regularly also are more likely to be responsible in paying child support as well as voluntarily buying things for the children, thereby alleviating a large portion of the mother's financial burden. Additionally, fears of the children being intensely hurt by the divorce are abated when the separation does not

Table 7.   Interrelation of Visitation Arrangement and the Areas in Which
Mothers Noted Differences in Reactions

Differences in Reactions	Chi Square	Level of Significance
Mother very lonely, children not or much less so	3.98	$p < .05$
Mother angry at father, child angry at both parents	5.76	$p < .02$
Children experience minor upset of brief duration, mother intensely upset	6.56	$p < .02$
Mother intensely hurt by father, felt rejected and very upset, not children	1.82	$.20 > p > .10$

result in the children truly losing regular contact with their father. The children's sense of vulnerability however, remains independent of the degree of contact with the father.

Table 8 shows the results of statistical analysis on the impact of the frequency of visitation on where children perceive differences. The impact of various visitation arrangements on a family's responses to divorce is clearly a complicated one. Both Wallerstein and Kelly (1974, 1975, 1976) and Jacobson (1978a) oversimplified the situation in their views. Wallerstein and Kelly's concentration on the necessity of a child being able to see his father several times a week at his convenience in order to be gratified by the postdivorce father-child relationship causes them to miss out on the other effects of differences in frequency of visitation. Likewise, although Jacobson's finding that the greater the loss of time with the father, the higher the "maladjustment of the child," is not contradicted, she leaves out totally the effect of visitation on the mother and hence on the relationship between the mother's and child's reactions.

Ways in Which the Reports of the Mothers and Children Are Dissimilar

A discussion of the ways in which a mother's report often differed from the information related in her child's interview began by focusing on the areas where mother and children see differences between their reactions. In general,

Table 8. Interrelation of Visitation Arrangement and the Areas in Which
Children Noted Differences in Reactions

Differences in Reactions	Chi Square	Level of Significance
Mother angry at father, not child	3.67	p < .10
Mother angry at father, not child plus child only a little	3.53	p < .10
Child angry at both parents about divorce, mother angry at father about a lot of things	4.00	p < .05
Child wanted reconciliation, not mother	2.23	.20 > p > .10
Mother has role in divorce, choosing it even if it makes her sad, child did not want it at all	3.10	p < .10
Child scared, mother not or much less so	3.14	p < .10
Child scared as well as mother but of different things	3.91	p < .05

two types of errors are common in a mother's or child's perceptions of how the
other is reacting. (The word "error" is used to describe all instances in which
one family member describes another's reactions in a contrary manner to how
he himself had described his reactions. This practice is based on the
assumption that, while a denial of certain reactions may be doubted, an
individual's assertion that he experienced a certain reaction provides the most
accurate assessment of what he felt.) Mothers and children both altogether
missed many of the reactions which the other experienced and, somewhat less
frequently, severely underestimated the intensity of the other's reactions.

The number of areas where mothers totally miss noticing their child's
reactions to the divorce process is indicative of severe gaps in a mother's
understanding of her children's behavior and feelings in the aftermath of a
parental separation. Most often, mothers failed to notice that their child was
angry at them because of the divorce, surprised by the divorce, uncomfortable
about letting peers know of the changes in their family, and afraid of so many

aspects of his future. While these misperceptions account for only a fraction more than one-third of the child sample, the percentage is large indeed when it is realized that these are not cases where the child responded in a certain way but rather where the mother did not see the child's response at all.

For between one-fourth and one-third of the mother-child pairs, the mother missed entirely that her child had been scared. In 13 of these cases, the child described himself as somewhat scared, mentioning a few different fears. In eight more, the child stated that he was extremely frightened and presented a long list of worries. Similarly, for over one-fourth of the children interviewed, the mother missed that her child had been angry at his father for getting divorced. Slightly less than one-fourth of the child sample was accounted for in instances where the mother missed that her child was lonely and that he questioned whether it was his fault.

In some instances, the mother did not totally miss that her child felt a certain way but yet described these reactions as occurring in a *much* milder form than the child himself reported. With regard to 14 children (21 percent of the child sample), the mother did not realize how much the child missed his father or the extent of the child's feeling of loss. In 12 instances (18 percent of the children), mothers stated that their children felt "fine" after just a very brief period of upset (e.g., by the next day) while their children said they were sad for a long time. Likewise, in 12 cases, the mothers reported that their child was slightly upset by the divorce. The child related turmoil and a feeling that his world had been turned topsy-turvy. Less frequently, mothers severely underestimated the intensity of their child's fears although recognizing some insecurity (10 children, 15 percent of the child sample) and the intensity of their child's anger, as well as the number of situations which the child resented (8 children, 12 percent of the child sample).

Children seem less likely than their mothers to miss totally such basic reactions as fear and anger but they often fail to grasp the various nuances of their mother's divorce experience. Thus, while describing how distressed and lonely their mother became, slightly over one-third of the children missed that their mother felt isolated from her former friends, unlovable and worthless, and overwhelmed by the extent of her responsibilities. Similarly, although children rarely stated incorrectly that their mother had no fears due to the divorce, between one-fourth and one-third of the children failed to recognize all of these fears. Between one-fourth and one-third of the children also missed that their mother felt rejected and hurt by their father, and guilty about the divorce, especially in relationship to its effect on them.

Three examples were seen where the child failed to recognize the intensity of the mother's response to the divorce. First, 13 children (19 percent of the child sample) observed that their mother had been unhappy during the divorce process but did not realize the strength of her depression. Second,

7 children (10.5 percent of the children) were not aware of how intensely angry their mother was at their father or that the anger was an ongoing feeling. Finally, another seven children severely underestimated how frightened their mother was of the changes that were taking place in her life.

Significance of These Discrepancies in Reports for Mothers and Children Helping Each Other with the Divorce

Most simply, if a mother is unaware that her child is feeling a particular way, she is likely to be unable to help him resolve that feeling. Furthermore, she is certainly incapable of being empathic about what the child is experiencing. The child must therefore cope with large aspects of the divorce mainly by himself and must deal with a mother, who at the very least has shown no inclination to share his difficulty.

In several instances, the mother's knowledge of the way the child was truly feeling would have allowed her to alleviate much of his distress. If a mother were more aware that her child missed his father or how intensely he longed to see him, she could arrange for more frequent contact between father and child and perhaps more actively push reluctant fathers into paying attention to their children. Her assumption that the children largely have an out of sight, out of mind mentality, leads her to a misguided contentment with the children's apparent calm between visits. Likewise, if she were aware of the children's loneliness or again, of its intensity, and her role in creating this feeling, she could work toward organizing her schedule so that the children remain alone less frequently.

At times, the mother's failure to recognize how her child is actually reacting may result in her creating a situation which is even harder for him to handle. For example, in several families where the mother assumed that her child picked up on the tension in the parents' predivorce relationship and proceeded to prepare himself for the eventual separation, the mother's failure to predict or even notice the child's surprise led her to minimize the need for thoroughly explaining the situation and preparing the child for all eventualities. Consequently, the child's confusion and fear are possibly increased.

Similarly, while the mother's failing to see some of the child's fears may result in specific areas where the child misses out on needed reassurance, a total lack of realization that the child has become frightened of what will take place in his future, especially of the permanence of his relationship with his parents, sharply intensifies the child's own stress and mother-child conflicts. The most obvious instance of this last problem occurs when the child manifests his fear that something dreadful will happen to his parents by becoming clingy or obnoxious when the mother makes plans to go out, or by being more irritable when the mother must leave for work or the child must stay with a babysitter after school. The mother, missing the fear underlying the child's behavior, makes little effort to remain home when it is possible or to provide him with the details of her outings which he requires to feel secure. Furthermore, she acts as if he is just making her life difficult and resents his negative behavior. The mother's impatience with his behavior in turn, escalates the child's already present fear of losing her. The mother may also wrongly conclude that the child resents her dating because she is becoming involved with new men as opposed to the possibility that the child is primarily concerned with being left alone.

Mothers who incorrectly report that their child was not angry at them regarding the divorce do not typically think that their child is never angry. Rather, they misinterpret the real reason for much of his angry behavior. Many mothers do not realize that just because their child has expressed anger in the past about something she did that bothered him, he is not necessarily comfortable revealing anger related to the divorce. The true cause of angry outbursts following the separation is therefore not probed and the child's behavior is understood as a series of isolated incidents requiring discipline rather than sympathy. It is possible that the failure of the mother to address the child's resentment of her for getting divorced is one reason why Wallerstein and Kelly discovered that anger does not easily abate after a parental separation.

Some effects of the mother's missing that the child, like her, was angry at his father were elaborated when the impact on family functioning of perceived differences in reactions was discussed. Primarily, this discussion focused on the friction which arises in the mother-child relationship when the mother perceives the child as being blind to his father's faults while she intensely resents much of his behavior. Certainly the mother and child's feelings are rarely identical with regards to the father but failing to see the aspects which are similar results in the mother thinking that her child is incapable of understanding her point of view.

The children interviewed commented both that they were upset and/or angered when their mother seemed glad the divorce was taking place and when she was depressed because of it. The impact on the child of his lack of awareness of certain reactions on the part of the mother is therefore far from simple. For example, failing to observe that his mother felt unlovable, isolated from friends, or rejected, may have interfered with the child's ability to understand her need to have a social life which excluded him and thus caused her to lose out on the support which would have eased her concerns and guilt. However, knowledge of these reactions would also have probably upset the child and increased his sense of insecurity regarding the permanence of his mother's presence and love. Likewise, while acknowledgment of the mother's financial worries and fears regarding the children seem to be taken as a matter of course, recognition of the full extent of the mother's fears would further shake the child's image of his mother as the strong figure in the family. This is a time when the loss of the daily presence of the father increases the importance of maintaining this image. Resentment of the mother's perceived contentment with the divorce would be lessened and empathy would be gained but these changes would occur at the price of intensifying the child's already existing worries.

The child's missing that his mother felt overwhelmed by her new responsibilities creates a situation more like the result of the mother missing out on the child's surprise or fear. Not only does he make no attempt to alleviate the mother's burden but he also commonly adds to it with increased demands. By misinterpreting the mother's fatigue or need for extra support (practical and emotional) as reflecting a disinterest in the child's feelings or anger at him, he also gets hurt and feels isolated when these responses are not truly warranted. In families where the mother reported feeling most overwhelmed, the children typically reported feeling unloved and being continually angry at her. The children's feelings in turn, increase the mother's sense of being overwhelmed, creating a cycle which is difficult to break.

Factors Leading to the Difficulty in Understanding the Other's Reactions

A major factor leading to the discrepancies between a mother's view of her children's reactions and their self-report is the unrealistic expectations which many mothers hold, before the separation, of how their children will respond to the divorce process. When mothers describe how they expected their children to respond to the news of the impending separation or the departure of their father, the reactions they anticipated are often melodramatic and typically include frequent explosive outbursts of anger or sadness. When these dreaded reactions do not occur, the mothers are greatly relieved. They also however, then tend to conclude that the children are finding it fairly easy to adjust to the divorce and that their unexpectedly calm demeanor signifies that no severe pain is experienced. The sharp contrast between the mother's portrayal in her own mind of what the divorce would do to the children and the reality of their responses leads her to confuse the meaning of their actual behavior. Relevant excerpts from two interviews which illustrate this finding are quoted below. In both cases, at least one of the children in the family demonstrated a great deal of upset during the interview, indicating that he had yet to cease reacting to the divorce. All the children commented that they had negative feelings when the separation first occurred. Both mothers clearly care a great deal about their children and were very concerned about hurting them.

I: And what about when you actually got divorced and your husband moved out. How did each of the kids react then?

M: *They, I asked them after he had been gone a couple of weeks, I said, how do you feel, and now that their dad was gone, and they said they really didn't think it was much different because the further we got into the divorce the less he was around. So they said it really doesn't seem that much different because dad wasn't home that much anyway. So I think it was a gradual getting into it for them, the fact that he was gone so much.*

I: Have you noticed any other reactions in them over the course of time or the ways that they've changed?

M: *Not really. I expected a lot more. I was expecting them to be more angry at everything and in general, than they have been. They really adjusted to it much better than I thought they would. I really haven't seen a whole lot of difference in them. I expected to see much more. In fact, I thought maybe they were denying it and so I thought I'll take them to counseling and I talked to a friend who is a counselor and he said as long as we could talk about it openly that I shouldn't worry about it, so I've been going along those lines. . . . They just seem to have accepted it so much that I am really surprised. I expected to see things that I had read about. I would think they would react more than they have.*

I: How do you feel about what you've described is going on with the kids?

M: *I feel glad that they've accepted it as well as they have because I was worried about that. That was one thing that kept me from filing for a long time. . . . I thought that there would be more outward actions and I thought they would be more upset with my husband and myself and they seem to have adjusted so well.*

I: What sorts of feelings came up for you when the kids reacted as they did?

M: *Well I think it, I was sort of worried that they were denying it. I just expected more fights and more towards me and towards each other, more animosity. I'm happy that they weren't feeling that way but on the other hand, I was worried that they were holding it in and I didn't think that was good.*

*   *   *

I: I was asking about your general feelings at this point about the divorce.

M: *Well, number one, the children are the most important thing to me and I think that I really would feel I had made a mistake if I felt the children were definitely suffering without him here. But I see and always did see that the separation's final and once it's over, that they're fine, they're doing fine.*

I: And you were worried that they wouldn't?

M: *Yes, that they might listen so much and cry and be depressed, lonely for him, and so on. But as soon as he left, the air around here was so much more relaxed and happy, the tension was gone and everyone wasn't uptight.*

I: Can you tell me how the kids reacted at the time when you told them about the divorce.

M: *Lou cried.... Now when I told Mark, who is a very sensitive child, he just looked at me and said okay.... It was just as if I were telling him today we're not going to the pool because it's too cold to go to the pool or something like that.*

I: Could you give me some sense of how each of the children reacted to the separation and then following the divorce, and how they've changed since then. Why don't you take Lou first.

M: *What do you mean?*

I: I'd like to get a sense of the different reactions that they had at different points.

M: *I'm drawing a blank. I'm having a difficult time answering.*

I: Well, why don't we take the first separation. How do you remember them reacting when you first separated?

M: *Oh there was an occasional question. Is Daddy coming over or is Daddy coming by. There wasn't a big deal. That's why I'm having a hard time pinpointing the reactions from the children.*

Wallerstein and Kelly (1980) noted another expectation on the part of the mothers which, although observed less frequently in this study than the one described above, also blurred the mothers' view of their children's reactions. Wallerstein and Kelly commented that parents often contend that "the experience of the children can be subsumed under the experience of the adults." That is, "that a marriage that is unhappy for the adults is unhappy for the children and, furthermore, that a divorce that promotes the happiness of the adults will inevitably benefit the children as well." A mother may perceive her children as relieved following the separation, when it is in fact she who is relieved. Similarly, she may believe that the children are actually more content or at least satisfied with their current degree of contact with their father because she finds the postdivorce situation a better one for herself. Both the research of Wallerstein and Kelly and the findings of the present study raise serious doubts about the validity of this type of viewpoint.

An additional factor which contributes to an individual's failure to recognize the reactions of other members of his/her family is a "hear no evil, see no evil, speak no evil" approach to dealing with the divorce. The children interviewed were more verbal about their adherence to this defensive approach but many mothers appeared to act on its premises as well. Child or mother would profess to know little about the other's feelings and also show little inclination to find out anything. Interview questions were greeted with a reluctance to even make guesses about what the other was feeling. No one in the family spoke spontaneously about the divorce and no one asked the other questions. The following are all responses from children participating in this study when asked about specific aspects of their mother's reaction or about their mother's overall feelings about the divorce.

> *I couldn't describe it 'cause she didn't tell me anything about that part.*

> *Well I don't really know that. I didn't know how she feels, if she's guilty or nothing 'cause she never usually tells us her problems or anything.*

> C: *I don't really know what her mother might feel. I didn't know what my mother felt because she really wouldn't tell us anything.*
> I: Did you ask her about it?
> C: *No, I didn't ask her about it.*

> *I can't really tell because I only know how upset I am.*

Adding to the lack of understanding of the other's reactions due to the just discussed reluctance to learn about what the other family members are feeling, was a tendency of many interviewees to hide their own reactions from the rest of the family. One reason behind this effort to avoid revealing any reaction to the divorce is a belief, corresponding to the one above, that if one avoids thinking about the divorce and acts like nothing has changed, the bad feeling will go away. Other thoughts also motivate this behavior however. Both mothers and children explained that they wished to protect the other family members from their reactions. Mothers commonly believed that it was inappropriate for the children to know the details of their pain or to burden them with such feelings as anger at their father. Likewise children, in particular those who perceive their mother to be severely depressed by the divorce, did not want her to be further upset by the knowledge that they too felt very bad. As described earlier, children often refrained from expressing anger for fear that it would be retaliated and that their mother or father would stop loving them as a result. Finally, individuals attempted to keep their feelings hidden because of an assumption that they were the only ones left in the family who were still reacting to the divorce process. Children often seemed embarrassed by this notion or worried that something was wrong with them because they just couldn't get accustomed to their father being gone.

Furthermore, given that they believed that their mother was totally content with her new life, they anticipated that verbalizing their feeling would result only in reproach or an unsatisfying response such as "this is the way things are." Since the child knows he is helpless to change the situation he sees nothing to be gained by discussing it.

In some instances, children appeared to have difficulty recognizing some of their mother's reactions because her feelings were beyond their comprehension. The children tended to perceive their mother so much in relationship to themselves that they were often unable to describe those reactions such as her feeling isolated or unlovable which stemmed from certain needs in relationships which existed totally separate from them and which they could not meet. It is also possible that a defensive need to regard their mother as strong, contributed to their maintaining an image of her which was inconsistent with seeing her, for example, as worthless and unlovable. Defenses likely play a role in the mother's misperceptions as well. Some mothers may need to believe that the children have adapted easily and possibly are benefitting from the divorce in order to resolve their own conflicts about getting a divorce. They deny any evidence which suggests the children are finding it difficult to cope with having separated or divorced parents.

Mothers in particular failed to notice what the rest of their family was feeling because they were too self-absorbed in their own efforts to cope with the divorce. They were often surprised during the interview when they tried to report what the children were feeling at the time of the separation and could only recall their own anger or depression:

> *How do I feel about what's going on with the kids? As I'm thinking about what the questions are that you've asked and what the answers were, some of my feelings are either I haven't been very aware of what their feelings are or that it hasn't really been that big a problem.*

M: *I don't know if I, I don't think he ever told them. He just said he was leaving. . . . I don't remember, I don't remember. Those days were just, they were all blurred for me. I don't even know.*

I: Did you talk to them at all about it, like when he first moved out?

M: *No. I didn't talk to them at all. I was in crying fits constantly.*

I: How have each of them reacted or changed since then: Why don't you take Andy first. What were the reactions that he had?

M: *I really can't even separate both of them. It's all very muddled. I think maybe they were relieved if I really tell the truth about it because we fought all the time. I think they think they have more of him, and more of his attention than when he was here. . . . I can't remember a definitive reaction from either one of them except they always seemed to take it better than I did.*

Impact of Sex, Sibling Order, and Visitation Arrangement on Where the Reports of Mothers and Their Children Differ

Contrary to predictions made prior to carrying out this research, sibling order appears to be the predominant factor affecting the mothers' tendency to describe the children's reactions to the divorce in a manner different from the children's self-reports. It affects the mother's ability to recognize both the existence of certain reactions and their intensity. In general, mothers seem to underplay the difficulty their older child has in coping with the changes the family is undergoing. The older sibling is assumed to have been more aware of problems prior to the divorce and thus more likely to accept the divorce easily and possibly even regard it as a well-chosen solution. Two significant findings and numerous trends which support this conclusion are demonstrated in an analysis of the data. In instances where the child reported that he/she was surprised by the news of the divorce while the mother reported otherwise, older siblings are represented twice as often as their younger sister or brother ($p < .10$). Furthermore, mothers perceived their older child as relieved by the separation when this was not the case (at least according to the child involved) much more often than their younger child ($p < .10$ after Yates's correction).

The number of mother-child pairs involved is too small for statistical significance to be demonstrated but with one exception, the remaining cases affected by sibling position manifest results in the same direction as above. When mothers missed entirely that their child was moderately frightened by the divorce, they referred to their older child about twice as often (nine older as compared with five younger). Likewise, mothers missed completely that their older child was hurt and sad because of the divorce process over two times as frequently as their younger child. In terms of underestimating the intensity of the child's responses to this crisis, mothers missed the degree of their child's upset much more often for their older child ($.20 > p > .10$). Additionally, they did not come close to realizing the extent of their child's anger four times as often with their older child. Finally, older children were represented over twice as often in cases where their mother did not see how frightened their child was by what was happening to his family (i.e., the mother reported that her child showed evidence of being scared but did not come close to realizing the strength of his fears).

The one exception to the rule is that in relationships where the child related that he had been angry about the divorce but the mother reported differently, younger children were discussed significantly more often than their older siblings ($p < .05$). Given that mothers fairly commonly remain oblivious to much or all of the anger of both of their children, a possible explanation for this particular finding is that the older sibling, when he is resentful of the divorce, is likely to be more verbal about his opposition to it.

They perceived greater lack of understanding of the problems which led to the separation on the part of the younger children is thus seen to lead to greater shock and sadness but not anger.

As stated earlier, sibling position was not considered by Wallerstein and Kelly to impact on the nature of the child's reaction to divorce and was not examined by other researchers. Wallerstein and Kelly did not consider whether sibling position affected the interrelationship of the mother's and child's reactions or changes in their relationship. Age of the child, as a factor influencing his responses and manner of coping, has received the most attention. Yet, here again, no one has really pursued the way age affects how a mother perceives or misperceives her child's reactions. In this study, the number of families interviewed is too small to tease apart the separate influence of age and sibling position on the interaction of different family members' feelings and behavior in response to the divorce process. However, since the age range of the child sample is relatively limited and the younger sibling in some families is older than the older sibling in others, sibling position seems to be an important variable in and of itself. The mothers participating in this research were clearly less likely to pick up on the pain their older child was experiencing. Since the older child is also the one more likely to be given greater responsibilities, one can assume that regardless of his actual age, he/she is regarded as altogether more competent. This view may result in the older child receiving less support in his efforts to adjust to the divorce and also being leaned on as a support for the mother. The results of statistical analysis regarding sibling position are reviewed in table 9.

The one area where the sex of the child was shown to influence significantly the outcome of analysis concerns the child missing his father. In this respect, the present research replicates the work of Wallerstein and Kelly. Mothers do not realize the extent of their child's longing for his father much more often when describing their sons ($\chi^2 = 4.27$, $p < 0.05$). This result seems to reflect the tendency of boys to miss their father's daily presence more intensely in conjunction with the tendency of mothers to play down this reaction.

One significant result of statistical analysis involving the impact on the mother's thinking of the visitation arrangement, was also discovered. Mothers are far more likely to completely miss that their child was hurt and sad when visitation is irregular ($\chi^2 = 5.12$, $p < .05$ after Yates's correction for small cell frequencies). In keeping with the discussion of the effect of visitation on where mothers see differences between their own reactions and those of their children, this finding again demonstrates that mothers often fail to recognize how much children are upset by the loss of regular contact with their father and how much the frequency and predictability of visitation affects the speed with which a child adjusts to the divorce.

Table 9.   Interrelation of Sibling Position and a Mother's Failure to
Perceive Accurately Her Child's Reactions

Nature of Misperception	Chi Square*	Level of Significance
Child surprised, mother thought not	3.26	p < .10
Mother says child felt relieved, child says no	3.48	p < .10
Child somewhat scared, mother misses this entirely	1.41	N.S.
Child very hurt and sad, mother did not see this at all	1.14	N.S.
Mother missed degree of child's upset	2.48	.20 > p > .10
Mother says child was angry but does not come close to realizing the intensity of the child's anger or how many aspects of the situation the child is angry about	1.54	N.S.
Mother misses to large extent how frightened her child was	1.14	N.S.
Mother misses entirely her child's anger at her	4.48	p < .05

*In all but the last misperception listed, the direction of the impact of sibling position is the same: a mistake was made far more frequently in describing the older child in a family.

Overall, none of the variables under consideration impact greatly on where children misperceive their mother's reactions. The only significant findings pertain to the influence of the visitation arrangement. Two areas of impact are shown, both indicating that children are less aware of their mother's difficulty when they have regular frequent contact with their father. First, in instances where the mother related that she was hurt and rejected by her ex-husband while the child appeared totally unaware of this, children with regular visitation outnumbered those with irregular visitation 12:3 ($\chi^2 =$

3.996, p < .05). It seems that when the children do not feel rejected by their father and witness their parents carrying out what is best for them, they have trouble seeing that their mother does not feel she has been treated equally as well. Second, children with regular visitation missed that their mothers felt overwhelmed almost three times more frequently than children with irregular visitation ($\chi^2 = 3.858$, p < 0.05). Again, as above, children do not realize that their mother can have so much difficulty coping when their father remains actively in the picture. They are apparently unable to separate out his ability to be supportive of them from his lack of ability to be supportive of their mother.

It had been predicted that mothers and children would be more attuned to each other when visitation was consistently frequent. This expectation was based on the notion that regular visitation made it likely that the parents were cooperative with each other and postdivorce life was progressing relatively smoothly. The above results however, suggest that regular visitation may in fact, partially blur the children's view of their mother's difficulty coping with the loss of her husband.

In conclusion, an examination of the interrelationship of mothers' and children's reactions to divorce reveals that a family's coping with the aftermath of parental separation is a complex process. While it is important to understand how individual children and adults respond to this crisis, a focus on the individual is not enough. Certain patterns of family response such as the mother perceiving her feelings related to anger as vastly different from her son's or a failure on the part of many mothers to realize how unprepared her children were for the news of the separation also need to be studied if the goal of the mental health professional is to plan the best possible preventive and clinical interventions.

9

A Family Copes with Divorce

Each individual brings to the divorce situation his/her own responses to the events which take place and to the reactions of other family members. Divorce creates stress for mothers and children both because of the nature of the individual reactions and because of the strain these reactions place on family relationships.

Central to the mothers' divorce experience is overwhelming pain and severe narcissistic injury. The women described their self-absorption during the divorce process as they attempted to cope with their varying intense emotions. Similarly, they detailed their belief that they were worthless and unlovable. They wondered if the marriage failed because they were inadequate in some way, and doubted their desirability to any man. A great deal of anger was also evident in the mothers' reports. It can be assumed that this anger resulted from the mothers' desire to lash out at the husband who hurt them so much. Yet, in contrast to their open explanations of their depressed feelings, the mothers were usually very uncomfortable revealing their anger. Their rage at their ex-husband remained largely unexpressed: the mothers frequently limited their discussion of anger to ways in which the husband's behavior negatively affected their children and thus infuriated them.

Indications of more intense anger were apparent indirectly however. Despite the fact that only four mothers recognized that rage at their ex-husband was in part displaced to their children, the reports of the children, and the mothers' discussion of other aspects of their divorce experience, suggest that this was the case. The children stated that their mother was crabby and on edge, and revealed that she often unpredictably became angry at them. In describing their guilt and fears, the mothers concentrated on feelings related to the children. The women's conscious understanding of these feelings consisted of concerns that the events of the divorce would cause their children pain and hamper healthy development. It is likely that underlying these concerns were guilt and anxiety stemming from their own destructive impulses toward the children displaced from their ex-husband. Given that the mothers expressed far more worry about their sons than their daughters, it can be assumed that boys were commonly the object of the mothers' displaced rage and thus the focus of much internal conflict.

The mothers' difficulty dealing with their children postdivorce does not result solely from displaced aggression. Mothers often spoke of how they felt pulled between their wish to meet the perceived needs of their children and their desire to engage in a social and professional life which excluded the children. The practical issue of dealing alone with the enormous demands of maintaining a house and attending to the daily tasks of childrearing added to the mothers' sense of being over-burdened and caused them to be impatient and short-fused. Finally, the children's anger at their mother in the aftermath of the separation, which the women frequently regarded as largely undeserved, and their continuing love for their father and hope for a reconciliation, create considerable pressure which increases the mothers' tendency to have hurtful impulses toward the children.

The children's reactions to the divorce process contribute to the tension in the mother-child relationship. At odds with the mothers' efforts to withdraw emotional investment in their ex-husband, the children miss their father terribly and long for his return. The loss of the father's daily presence and the breakup of the family unit threaten the children's positive sense of themselves and their world. The children's lowered self-esteem was reflected in the interviews in numerous accounts of their reluctance to let anyone know of the divorce and their feeling that they were now different from their friends. In explaining their expectation that they would be ostracized, they talked as if their father no longer existed, revealing how they experienced his absence. The children's shaky sense of the world was seen chiefly in their elaboration of extensive fears which emerged following the separation. They indicated concern that their father would be separated from them completely or stop loving them. Similarly, although to a lesser extent, they worried that their mother too would abandon them. Fears of the future abounded. For example, the mothers' concerns about finances were often translated into anxiety about the terrible fate which would befall them when the money ran out.

A common method of defending against the intense feeling of loss is idealizing the predivorce father-child relationship. Interactions prior to the separation were frequently described in an unbalanced rosy manner. This idealization, as well as the more realistic desire to preserve a positive visitation relationship, excludes the possibility of the child fully expressing his rage at his father for leaving the family. Often, the highly ambivalent feelings toward both parents during the divorce process are split so that the custodial mother becomes the chief object of the child's anger. She alone is blamed for the breakup of the family. However, many children are also clearly in conflict about their anger toward their mother. In an effort to disown their hurtful impulses, the children may externalize their rage. This defense causes the anxiety arising from a shaken trust in their parents' commitment to their well being to escalate. During their interviews the youngsters thus presented long lists of the many ways in which their parents might be killed or maimed.

When placed in a family context, it can be seen that the individual reactions of mothers and their children do not mesh smoothly. At a time when all family members need help in rebuilding self-esteem and trust, conscious and unconscious anger impede positive interaction. Mutual fears of the other being hurt or driven away by this anger, as well as a belief that no one else still shares the pain, discourage open expression of these strong feelings. Furthermore, the essentially different attitudes with which most mothers and their children approach the divorce and the different intrapsychic tasks which they must accomplish (i.e., mothers need to decathect completely their ex-husband while children need to protect and alter their relationship with their father) serve largely to isolate the individual family members in their efforts to resolve their difficulties.

In the view of the women interviewed for this study, the differences between the mothers' and children's reactions, just described, were most notable between mothers and sons. In sharp contrast to their own feelings of anger toward their ex-husband, the women perceived their sons as either not angry at either parent about the divorce or angry solely at the mother, far more often than was the case when referring to their daughters. It is likely that the mothers' belief that boys more frequently idealize their father and unfairly blame their mother for the divorce, combined with the earlier mentioned tendency of mothers more commonly to displace rage at their ex-husband to their son, leads them to become less supportive of their sons following the separation. The boys' expressed sense of having lost their only ally when their father left home may thus result from a realignment in some families in the aftermath of divorce in which the females link together against the remaining male.

The stress created by the incompatability of the individuals' reactions is complicated by a failure of mothers and children to perceive accurately the reactions of the other family members. Although the women ranged considerably in their perceptiveness, there was a general tendency for mothers to overplay the importance of their role in the child's divorce experience. Perhaps because of their own efforts to end the attachment to their ex-husband or the fear that the children would reject them for their father, they denied the central position still held by the father, or more accurately, the loss of his daily presence. For example, loneliness was primarily attributed to the mothers' inability to spend as much time with the children as they had before the separation rather than the combined loss of time, and changed relationship, with both parents. Statistical analysis reveals that, in keeping with the above finding, the mothers were more likely to miss completely that their children were hurt and sad when visitation was irregular. The women clearly did not recognize the importance of frequent and predictable visitation for the child's postdivorce adjustment. Relatedly, the mothers frequently viewed their children's reactions as more similar to their own responses than actually appeared to be the case. They did not typically realize how much the children missed their father, how unprepared the children were for the events which transpired, or how long the children held hopes of a reconciliation.

Overall, both mothers and children underestimated the scope and intensity of the other's responses to the divorce process. Because of the mothers' defensive need to minimize the children's responses and the children's defensive need to hide many of their feelings, the women misinterpreted their children's outward acceptance of the divorce. While clearly recognizing the children's initial upset, the mothers failed in many instances to observe the children's continuing pain and showed little understanding of their anger, fear, and confusion. This situation was most pronounced with regards to the mother's view of her older child. It was demonstrated that mothers misperceived the older sibling as expecting the divorce and being relieved by it significantly more often than they misread the reactions of the younger child.

Children similarly presented a defensively distorted report of their mother's divorce experience. They indicated that their mother was distressed, lonely, angry, and afraid but frequently did not understand the extent of her depression and anxiety, or how overwhelmed she felt by the pressures of single parenthood. In fact, except in cases when the mother's reaction was extremely severe, the children depicted their mother as adjusting fairly rapidly and largely happy and/or relieved about the divorce. This unrealistic view was maintained during the interview through the use of wide-spread denial as the children claimed to have only very limited knowledge of their mother's feelings following the separation. The recognition of their mother as depressed, insecure, and less capable, as well as thoughts of becoming contagiously overwhelmed by her negative feelings provoked anxiety for the children.

Additionally, an egocentric orientation combined with a cognitive concreteness led the children to miss reactions such as the mother's sense of isolation, which were not evident through daily mother-child interactions. Egocentrism also resulted in misinterpretation of some of the mother's behavior, particularly her moodiness and angry outbursts toward the children. Failing to see that the anger stemmed, in part, from being overwhelmed and depressed or that the mother was expressing anger which originated from feelings toward her ex-husband, the children simply asserted that their mother's attitude toward them had changed. Their loneliness, fears, and sense of loss were consequently increased.

In conclusion, it can be seen that divorce is a crisis situation both for the individuals involved and their relationship as a family. Further research is clearly needed so that the long-term impact of the reactions elaborated in this study can be learned. It is evident however, that the mothers' and children's fears and anger, as well as their lack of insight into each other's feelings, work against a quick resolution to the problems which arise. Of particular concern with regards to healthy child development, are the implications for troubled separation during adolescence due to conflicts in feelings toward both parents and the resulting difficulty in incorporating positive identifications. Changes in the mother's view of her children, especially her tendency to treat her daughter as her ally and/or her older child as a second adult, contribute to a reluctance to support moves toward separation and further complicate the child's predicament.

Appendix A

Methodology

Sample

Guidelines for Selecting the Sample

In recognition of the likely influence of variables such as age and length of time since separation on the outcome of this research, an attempt was made to restrict the sample in a number of ways. Only families comprised of a mother and two children, who had experienced a divorce in the last nineteen months were asked to participate. At least one of the two children had to be within the targeted age range of seven through thirteen years of age. The sample was further defined by being limited to families in which custody had been granted to the mother, the separation preceding the divorce had not exceeded eighteen months and the divorce was the first for both parents. Additionally, in order to avoid the possibly confounding variable of severe economic hardship, families with predivorce incomes below $14,000 were eliminated from the sample population.[1] With the same goal in mind, it was initially planned that women who had remarried would not be included. However, as soon as the first two mothers were contacted, and the interviewer was informed that they had a boyfriend living with them, this decision was reversed. It was felt that a failure to include women who had a legal live-in arrangement would simply result in the avoidance of one segment of the divorced population and thus skew the sample towards those who remained single for a longer period. Remarriage, although certainly recognized as presenting some unique issues, may now be seen more as one end of a continuum (with "no dating" at the other) than as a totally separate circumstance.

The family constellation described above was chosen as the focus of study for several reasons. First, since meaningful comparison to Wallerstein and Kelly's research was desired, an effort was made to duplicate one of their subsamples. Latency and preadolescent children comprised the largest group they studied. As discussed earlier, when dividing their sample of 131 children, aged two and-one-half to eighteen years, into subgroups according to the

typical reactions of the children, Wallerstein and Kelly separated these
youngsters into only two groups whose reactions overlapped considerably.
Although the age of a few of the youngest children in the sample population
for this study would fall slightly below the cutoff for Wallerstein and Kelly's
early latency category, the remainder of the current sample corresponds to
that of Wallerstein and Kelly's early and late latency groups. That is, almost
all of the children interviewed for this research were aged six to twelve when
their parents first separated.

Second, children in this age range are old enough to understand the
interview questions designed for this research but are not yet oriented toward
separating from their family. This latter situation was avoided because the aim
of this project was to study children who had to resolve their feelings about
their parents' divorce within the context of their family and the requisite close
relationship with the custodial parent. It was felt that adolescents, knowing
they would be leaving home shortly, could cope with the divorce by biding
their time until they were independent of both parents.

Finally, Wallerstein and Kelly's observations that latency and
preadolescent children have the hardest time adjusting to their parents'
divorce and that the parent-child relationships for this age group were
especially troubled, make it important to examine these children's experience
more closely.

This sample differs from that of Wallerstein and Kelly in one significant
way. As stated earlier, they attempted to select a sample of "normal" children
by eliminating youngsters with a history of psychological problems. However,
given that they relied on referrals to a "Divorce Counselling Service" to obtain
their subjects the representativeness of their sample for the general divorce
population is questionable. The sample investigated in this study is truly
representative of the county population from which it was drawn. It is derived
from the divorce population as a whole and includes a few children who have
been in therapy for several years and many who were never seen as needing
psychological help of any sort.

Procedure for Obtaining the Sample

The process by which the sample interviewed for this study was achieved is
depicted in figures 1 and 2.

Because the number of subjects gathered through this sampling
technique failed to meet the desired total of 40 families, the researcher's
original plan only to interview families in which both children were within the
targeted age range was modified. As illustrated in figure 2, the sample was
enlarged to include families in which just one of the two children was between
the ages of seven years, zero months (7-0) and thirteen years, eleven months
(13-11).[2]

Figure 1. Sampling Flow: Part I

| | Records of divorces granted in Washtenaw County, October 1977–June 1979 |

↓

| Narrowing of sampling population possible through State files of vital statistics | Records of divorced families with two children, for which the duration of the separation was less than 18 months, the divorce was the dissolution of the first marriage for both husband and wife, and both children were between the ages of 7-0 and 13-11. |

↓

| Narrowing of sampling population possible through County court files: potential subjects | List of families included above in which the mother had sole custody of the children and the predivorce annual family income exceeded $14,000. Total = 53 families |

↓

| 58.5 percent of the potential subjects | List of families included above for which a current telephone number could be obtained—actual contact was made in all instances. Total = 31 families |

↓

| 83.9 percent of the families contacted consented to participate | Families which participated in the study. Total = 26 families |

Figure 2. Sampling Flow: Part II

Records of divorces granted in
Washtenaw County,
October 1977–April 1979

↓

Records of divorced families with
two children, for which the
duration of the separation was
less than 18 months, the divorce
was the dissolution of the first
marriage for both husband and
wife, and one child was between
the ages of 7–0 and 13–11.

↓

Potential subjects

List of families included above in
which the mother had sole
custody of the children and the
predivorce annual income
exceeded $14,000.
Total = 33 families

↓

57.6 percent of the potential
subjects

List of families included above for
which a current telephone number
could be obtained—actual contact
was made in all instances.
Total = 19 families

↓

73.7 percent of the families
contacted consented to participate

Families which participated in the
study.
Total = 14 families

Participation in this research was requested through a telephone contact. During this initial conversation, all mothers first heard the same speech and then were given the opportunity to discuss any concerns they might have. After an introduction, the speech focused on the purpose of the project (i.e., the need for understanding what all families dealing with the aftermath of divorce experience so that appropriate therapeutic and preventive measures can be designed for families desiring help). The importance of everyone's participation was emphasized. The interview procedure and what would be required of each person was then explained. Subjects were contacted at a time when appointments for the near future could be made. As is evident in figures 1 and 2, the refusal rate was extremely low. Overall, 80 percent of the women who were asked to take part in the study agreed for their family to be interviewed.[3]

Characteristics of the Actual Sample

The final sample consisted of 26 families with two children of latency or preadolescent age and 14 families with one child in this age range. In all cases the second child in the latter group was no older than fifteen or younger than three years of age. Overall, boys and girls are fairly evenly represented. The sample consisted of 31 boys and 35 girls.

Not surprisingly, one result of limiting the age of the children studied was a narrowing of the age of the adult sample. Over three-fourths of the mothers interviewed were in their thirties. The similarity in the age of most of the mothers rules out the possibility that large variations in age could account for differences in the women's reactions in divorce.

The design of the study limited the period of time which had elapsed since the parents' divorce to approximately a year and a half. The divorces for the actual sample occurred between five and nineteen months before the interviews for this research took place. No families were included in which the divorce occurred more recently than five months for two reasons. First, data were unavailable in the Department of Public Health for two months after the divorce was granted. Second, the interviewer delayed contacting more recently divorced families so that the sample would be more uniform with regards to the time factor. As is evident in table 10 the families were fairly evenly distributed across the fourteen-month time span in which divorces were granted.

Table 10.   Time Elapsed since Divorce

Time, in Months	Number of Families	Percent of Sample
5	1	2.5%
6–9	11	27.5%
9–12	8	20.0%
12–15	9	22.5%
15–18	8	20.0%
19	3	7.5%

It has already been shown that this sample represents the portion of the divorce population which is relatively stable geographically. It is unknown in what ways this fact prevents generalizing the findings of this study to all families who have experienced a divorce. Given that many mothers stated that they remained in their marital home or at least within the school district for the sake of the children (they believed that problems stemming from the divorce should not be compounded by a move to an new area) the current sample may be more attuned to children's needs. These mothers may also cope differently with the divorce than women who choose to move to an altogether different place and start anew. However, an assumption that this sample differs vastly from the group of families who moved out of town would be erroneous. Almost one-third of the families studied (i.e., 32.5 percent) had experienced a move since the parents separated, albeit within the county or its environs. In a few cases, the family had moved more than once: Stated reasons for the moves were most often economic ones. Four other families were seriously contemplating a move at the time of the separation; all were planning to leave Michigan. Furthermore, five fathers had moved to another state, thereby creating the same distance between the children and their father that the family's moving would effect.

Table 11 shows the distribution of the sample according to geographic location. The order of the sample in terms of the number of families in each area corresponds to the actual order of the towns in terms of the size of their population. At the time of the interviews, the largest number of subjects lived in Ann Arbor, a city with approximately 100,000 residents (U.S. Bureau of the Census, *Statistical Abstract of the United States: 1982–83*). A large portion of the city's population is employed by The University of Michigan. While this was true for several of the ex-husbands of the women in this sample, very few of the mothers presently work in a university-related position. Rather they are typically employed by a small business or a local professional. Ypsilanti is a somewhat smaller urban area whose major employer is a large automobile factory. A majority of the subjects residing in Ypsilanti worked on the assembly line at this factory. Saline is the largest of the small towns

Table 11.   Geographic Distribution of the Sample

Home	Number of Families	Percent of Sample
Ann Arbor	17	42.5%
Ypsilanti	11	27.5%
Saline	5	12.5%
All others	7	17.5%

surrounding Ann Arbor. It is basically suburban in appearance with many of the residents commuting to Ann Arbor for work. The remainder of the sample comes from the several small rural towns that comprise the rest of Washtenaw County, rural areas lying just outside county boundaries, and a city in Wayne County.

Research Design

The Research Instrument

Data for this study were collected by means of individual interviews with mothers and their children (i.e., those between the ages of 7-0 and 13-11 years). Interviews took place in the family's home with the aim of making everyone as relaxed as possible. The interview with the mother usually took between one and one-half and two hours to complete. However, if two hours elapsed without all the prepared questions being asked, the interview was left unfinished. The interview with the children typically lasted for forty-five minutes to one hour. In most cases, the entire family's interviews were completed in one visit. In half of the cases, the primary investigator interviewed the mother while another clinician interviewed the children. In the remaining families, the primary investigator interviewed both mother and children. Interviews were tape recorded and later transcribed.

The interviews were designed to tap those issues which were seen as most central to the particular mothers and children who took part in this research and also to address specific concerns of the researcher. They were thus conducted in a semistructured fashion. Both the adult and child interview schedule progressed in each of several sections from open-ended to more structured questions. The structured questions focused on those reactions reported by researchers in the past and also on the interviewer's interest in how family members respond to each other's reactions to the divorce. Certain issues such as anger which were anticipated to be difficult to discuss, were approached from several directions with the hope that the interviewee would become more open as he/she became more comfortable with the interview situation. In general, the format of the interview allowed the investigator to learn both what individuals will spontaneously reveal (and simultaneously what issues they will avoid) and how they will react when new thoughts are introduced.

In both the adult and the child interviews an effort was made to engage the interviewee in helping the researcher by regarding him/her as an "expert" in the area of divorce. Several questions were thus posed in terms of what the subject would tell another mother or child involved in the initial stages of a divorce process. For the child interviews a further step was taken to increase the likelihood of the youngster revealing an accurate picture of his divorce experience. In the sections of the interview concerned with the individual responses of both the child and his/her mother, including their reaction to each other's reactions, a large majority of the questions utilized displacement. Questions were asked in the third person and focused on the expected feelings of a boy/girl "a little younger" than the subject, or mothers in general. It was believed that the use of "displaced questions" would alleviate the tendency of latency and preadolescent children to invoke defenses common to this developmental stage such as reaction formation, intellectualization, and denial. This displacement was not rigidly maintained however. If the child repeatedly responded in the first person and, in the interviewer's judgment, appeared more comfortable in dealing directly with divorce-related issues, or if the child was, in fact, confused by the wording of the question, the use of displacement was dropped.

The interviews were piloted with four families before the sample for the study was contacted. In each case, the pilot subjects were similar to the families eventually included in the sample except for one factor which forced them to be excluded. For example, one women had been married twice while another had been separated longer than 18 months prior to her divorce. After each set of interviews, the interview schedules were revised to modify or eliminate questions which seemed especially confusing or failed to tap the feelings intended. Copies of the final versions of both the adult and child interviews are included in appendices B and C.

A Critical Look at the Research Instrument

An interview, especially one which allows for variations based on clinical decisions, has definite drawbacks as a research instrument. Interpretation of the data is subject to examiner bias so that reliability is uncertain. Additionally, since results are based solely on the self-report of the family concerned, inferences must be severely curtailed. This particular study is further compromised because much of the data gathered is retrospective in nature. The amount of time which has elapsed since many of the events of interest have occurred increases the possibility that responses reflect, at least in part, defensive distortions of an individual's divorce experience rather than an accurate recalling of past feelings and attitudes.

Despite the above limitations however, it was felt that at present, this sort of open-ended research was what was most needed in studying divorce. Wallerstein and Kelly's efforts to establish norms for mothers' and children's reactions to the divorce process and to develop a picture of what individuals and families experience were important to continue. An interview was chosen as the means for collecting data, rather than a questionnaire because it was felt that it presented greater opportunity to obtain an accurate understanding of a person's divorce experience. An interview allows flexibility in following up issues which appear to be important to a respondent. Given that the interviewer was an experienced clinician, she was able to assess the mother or child's response on the spot, including where defenses were predominant, and probe accordingly. The obvious added benefit of observing the individual's facial expression and body posture while the various aspects of divorce were discussed aided an understanding of interviewee responses. Moreover, the personal contact inherent in an interview and the encouraging support of the investigator were believed to increase the likelihood of a respondent becoming more revealing. Finally, whereas in a questionnaire, questions must be simplified so that no assistance in answering is necessary, an interviewer can explain any issues which seem confusing to the particular mother or child, and correct misunderstandings as they occur. Issues can therefore be addressed in a more complex and thereby, more realistic, manner.

Within the limitations of an interview study, an attempt was made to avoid some of the shortcomings of similar earlier research. First, the interview schedule was semistructured and consistently followed in all cases. Subjects were presented with more constant stimuli, making meaningful comparisons between families and replication of the overall study possible. Additionally, in recognition of the need for relying solely on what an individual consciously feels and chooses to report, data analysis remained largely focused on the view of the divorce process elaborated by the families themselves.

Appendix B

Mother Interview Schedule

Introduction

I'm meeting with you today so I can learn what divorce has been like for you and your kids. It is my hope that by talking to people who have experienced a divorce, we will better understand the process and be able to help people and make it less stressful in the future. I'm not here to judge how you've done nor in any way assess your adjustment or the kids' adjustment. I also do not want to poke into areas you feel are too personal to discuss so if a question feels that way please tell me. What I will be asking about is fairly complex. I want to talk about the reactions you've been having, the reactions the kids have been having, and how you affect each other. I realize that there are lots of feelings and reactions, not one set, and that these change over time. During the interview, don't feel hesitant if you think of other issues which you feel are important—we can always get back later to the questions I've prepared.

What you and the kids tell me today is totally confidential. I'm not related to the courts in any way. I also will not be contacting your ex-husband. No one else outside the project will see the materials either. Moreover, if there is anything written, it will not bear your names. The final write up of the study will not be reported by individuals, but rather by groups—how groups of people in your situation live with the shifts and changes following divorce. For example, we might talk about how boys as a group tend to react but not how a specific boy reacted. When the research is finished, I will send you a summary of my findings. Again, these will not be reported individual by individual. If you have any questions during the interview please interrupt me. Likewise, please feel free to contact me anytime after the interview. Okay?

Asking about Reactions

A. Mother's reactions

Could you first describe how you reacted to the prospect of divorce when you were first considering it?

How did you react at the time of the final separation and then to the divorce itself when it occurred?

How do you feel about it now?

What would you tell other women are the toughest things they'll have to face?

What would they be likely early on to worry about unnecessarily?

From your own experience, what should they be concerned about?

What can they do to make the divorce a lot better?

What might they do which would make the divorce much worse than it needs to be?

Let me now ask you about a couple of other things that come up with some people and not with others, and see how they apply to you. Have you had times when you felt _____? (or) when you were surprised at how _____ you felt? (Mention only those which subject has not referred to earlier.) E.g., you were unlovable or even really worthless, lonely, regretful, very angry, afraid about the future, guilty for getting divorced, euphoric, your moods really shifted a great deal, need to justify the divorce, isolated from other people, you found yourself missing your ex-husband, overwhelmed with all your responsibility, unprepared for the divorce or what followed, distrustful of new relations.

Have you ever found yourself trying to develop explanations as to what went wrong? What are they like?

B. Mother's View of Children's Reactions

Let's shift now to talking about your kids. How were the children told of the divorce?

How did they react to the news?

Can you give me a sense of how each of the kids have reacted or changed since then? Let's take _____ first. (If this isn't made clear:) In what ways are the kids' reactions different from each other?

You know your kids best. What are your notions as to why they have reacted differently? (Supply specifics if necessary.)

When x feels badly, what does he do to make himself feel better? What about y?

I'd again like to ask you a few specific things to see if these also apply to your kids. Have either of them felt _____? E.g., that dad was rejecting them when he left home, afraid that you would leave too, afraid of what might happen to your family, depressed, lonely, surprised, hopeful that you and your ex-husband would get back together, helpless, that they missed their father a lot, angry at you, angry at their father, that they couldn't show anger, torn between you and their father, ashamed with friends, more grown up, relieved by the divorce.

Kids react to change in different ways. Have you noticed if either of them have.... E.g., become less moody, more reluctant to go out, sad or angry if you go out, become more irritable, become calmer, started getting into fights at school, had some trouble doing their schoolwork.

Any other major changes that are especially worth noting?

Mother's Reactions to the Way the Children Are Reacting and Vice Versa

A. How do you feel about what you have described is going on with the kids?

(If necessary:) What sorts of feelings came up for you when the kids reacted in the way that they did?

(If necessary:) How did it make you feel when x _____? (Fill in major reactions.)

B. When you saw x doing _____ (or realized he was feeling _____) how did you manage it, what did you do?

What does x do now that upsets you?

What does x do now that gets you worried about him/her?

What does x do now that makes you angry?

What does x do now that makes you feel really good? (Same for y.)

C. What do you think has been the toughest thing for the kids?

What's been the toughest thing for you to explain to the kids?

What are the things that have been hard for you to deal with of the kids' reactions? What comes close to impossible?

What kinds of ways have you found yourself handling _____? (What she just mentioned.)

D. In thinking about the future, in what ways do you think the divorce will affect the kids?

(If necessary:) I've got a good picture now of the next few years, how about longer term? (Or use the reverse.)

E. In the same way I've asked you about your reactions to the kids' reactions, now I'd like to know what you make of how they have reacted to what you've been going through? (Again, supply specifics if necessary.)

What have they said or done that shows you how they are reacting to you? (If mother does not separate the kids ask if there are any differences between them in this regard.)

Mother-Child Relationship

A. How do you feel your relationship to each child has changed since you and your ex-husband separated?

Why do you think it has changed that way?

Again I'd like to ask you about some specifics. Sometimes after divorce there are changes in the way children are disciplined, is this true in your family? How has it affected your relationship to the kids?

There also may be changes in the way mothers and children show they care about each other, does this apply to your family? In general, do you feel closer or less close to your children? What has caused these changes?

Do you talk to one or both of your children about different things than you would have before you were separated?

Do you expect your children to take on more responsibility? act more adult? (I.e., change stemming from father not being present, how that affects your relationship to your children.)

B. (If not mentioned:) Are there any differences in your relationship to x and y? Has your relationship to x changed in a different way than your relationship to y?

What do you think these differences can be attributed to?

Do you think the fact that x is older and y is younger affects things?

Do you think the fact that x and y are boys/girls (or) Do you think the fact that x is a boy and y is a girl affects things?

(If the children are both of the same sex:) How do you think things might have been different if you had two boys/girls instead?

What things does x or y do now which you used to do?

What things does x do for y which you used to do?

Sibling Relationship

A. We've talked about how things have been for you and between you and your kids. Now let's talk about how things have been between your kids.

What were the children like with each other before the divorce? Ask about the following dimensions: sharing vs. jealousy, doing things together or more separately, degree of anger or rivalry, clear younger and older roles or more as peers on same level, general closeness vs. distance.

What's changed since the divorce?

B. Since the divorce your family has changed from a foursome to a threesome. How has that threesome changed? (or) How do you see yourselves reacting as a threesome now?

What's changed in the way you all relate as a family since the divorce process started?

Relationship to Father

A. How much contact do the children have with their father and what sort of contact is this? Has this been true since the divorce?

B. What's your best sense of what the kids feel about Dad now?

How has Dad's relationship to the kids changed since you two separated?

How are they reacting to their changed relationship with him?

What, if anything, looks different now than it did immediately after the separation? Immediately after the divorce?

C. How have you found yourself reacting to the way the kids feel now about Dad?

What's it like now when all four of you are together even if it's only for a moment? How is that different than it was at the time of the divorce?

What are the biggest gaps in the kids' lives because Dad is not here? Where has it made the most difference?

How does he still act toward them as he always did?

How is he still active in their daily lives? (If she has difficulty with this ask about specifics such as discipline, sharing daily events, teaching them skills, acting as a support, etc.)

D. Financial issues aside, what kinds of special problems does he now present for you or your relationship to the kids?

Are there ways he is a help?

What things do x or y do now for you or your family which their dad used to do?

E. What aspects of dealing with the kids is harder or hardest now that their father is gone?

What is easier or easiest?

F. I know that this might not be all known to you but to what extent has your ex-husband started seeing other women?

To what extent are the kids aware of that? To what extent do they interact with the kids?

How do the children react to it?

How do you feel about their reactions?

Same for the mother (unless she is remarried, then skip to next section). (If new person:) What functions or new roles in the family does this person (or people) play?

Did you ever talk about him with the kids? What did you say?

(If mother *has remarried* include this section)

How was your husband introduced to the children?

When was that? At what point in your relationship was that?

What were their reactions when they first met him?

How did they get to know him?

Did you ever talk about him with the kids? What did you say?

What do you think the kids felt when you first told them you were going to get married again?

How do you think the kids feel about it now?

How do you feel about their reactions?

What worried you the most about getting married again?

What is the relationship between the kids and their stepfather like?

In what ways has he taken on a father role? When did that happen?

What have been the best things for the family about you being married again?

What's been the hardest thing?

Did you date anyone else besides your present husband after separating from your first husband?

How did the children react to it?

How did you feel about their reactions?

To what extent did he/they get to know the children?

What functions or new roles in the family did this person play?

Changes in Environment, General Feelings

A. Have there been any other major changes recently besides the divorce? (E.g., move, change in mother's employment situation, mother return to school, financial situation.)

When did these occur?

How has each person reacted to them?

B. To whom have you turned for help since the decision to divorce? (Ask specifically about counseling if it is not mentioned.)

Have you felt that support for you has increased or decreased since the divorce?

Do you have different close friends than before the divorce?

What about the kids? Do they have new or increased contact with anyone in your extended family?

C. Some people view their divorce as an opportunity to change a lot of things in their family; others want to keep things the same as much as possible. Where along this continuum would you put yourself?

D. How do you feel about the decision to divorce now? for self? for whole family?

Appendix C

Child Interview Schedule

Introduction

We're talking to you today so we can learn about what it's like for kids when their parents get divorced. We need to understand what it's been like for you so we can make things better for other children. We won't be telling other kids what you say. In fact, we won't be telling anyone, not your mom, not your brother/sister, what you tell me. But, after we've talked to lots of kids and their moms we'll know much better how to help families during a divorce. Tracy, I will be asking your mom the same type of questions that I'll be asking you.

Asking about Reactions

A. Kid's reactions

How did you find out that Mom and Dad were going to get a divorce?

What did they say when they told you about it?

What were your feelings when that happened?

Let's suppose that I was trying to give advice to a boy/girl a little younger than you whose parents were going to get divorced. I want to help prepare him for what it's going to be like. What can I tell him are the sorts of feelings he will have about his parents getting a divorce?

What thoughts might he have when his father moves out of the house?

What thoughts might he have when the actual divorce happens?

How long will he feel that way until he really feels different?

What should I say are the hardest things he'll have to face?

What will he be likely to worry about?

What can he do to make things better? (If can't think of anything:) Is there really anything a kid can do to make things better? (If answers in terms of making the situation or his mother better:) What can he do to make himself feel better? (If answers in terms of making himself feel better:) What can he do to make things better for his family?

What might get nicer after the divorce?

How long did it take before you told your friends? Did you tell anybody right off?

How did you feel when you were telling them about the divorce?

Did you let your teacher know?

Okay, we've talked about lots of feelings, now I want to talk about a few more to see if you feel they might apply.

Do you think that someone might ever feel _____? Can you tell me more about that? (or) What would that be like? (Or other appropriate probes.) E.g., sad, lonely, afraid about what might happen to his family now, surprised, that he couldn't believe what was happening, miss Dad a lot, dream about Mom and Dad getting back together, that his Dad really didn't like him anymore, afraid Mom would leave too, angry at Mom, angry at Dad, feel he couldn't get angry or show he was angry, more grown up, relieved that they finally got divorced.

(Only ask about the reactions not spontaneously mentioned by the child in response to the previous questions.)

B.   Kid's view of mother's reactions

Now I'd like to talk about how mothers react to divorce. What could I tell someone his/her mom might feel when his/her parents *first decide* they're going to get a divorce?

How do you think she might feel *after* the divorce?

What do you think are the hardest things for moms about a divorce?

What might they be likely to worry about?

What things might get nicer for them?

What could a mom do to make herself feel better?

(For expected reactions not mentioned by the child:)

Do you think a mother might ever feel _____? How would she show that? (or) How would someone be able to tell she was feeling that? E.g., lonely, moody, very angry at Dad, still angry about the same things she was angry about before the divorce, guilty for getting divorced, really happy about the divorce, worried she might never get married again, worried about having enough money.

Now I'd like to talk about *your* family.

Does your mom ever seem like she's so involved in what she's thinking, she doesn't even notice some of the things going on at home?

Does your mom stay home more or go out more since the divorce? (If it logically follows:) Why do you think that's so?

What things does Mom call Dad about?

(If not mentioned:) What about when she has a problem?

How much does Mom mention Dad? What does she say?

Who in the family has been the most upset about the divorce?

How do they show how upset they are?

Who seems to have reacted the least?

Why do you think x has reacted the least?

Child's Reactions to the Mother's Reactions and Vice Versa

A. How would it make a child feel when his mom _____? (Fill in major reactions, if the child says that his mom goes out more be sure to ask how it makes him feel.)

What would he do about it?

B. What could a mom do that would upset her son/daughter?

What could a mom do that would get her son/daughter worried about her?

What might a mom do that would get her son/daughter really angry?

What might a mom do that would make her son/daughter feel really good?

What things might a mom say about the divorce or his/her dad which a kid just wouldn't want to hear?

What things might a kid wish his mom would tell him about the divorce? (I.e., What questions did you have about the divorce which mom hasn't *really* answered?)

C.   Sometimes, mothers and kids don't always feel the same way about the divorce. Sometimes, they don't feel the same way at the same time. Tell me about sometimes when you and your mom didn't feel the same way about the divorce.

(If the child can't answer the preceding question:) When Mom feels glad she got a divorce and you feel sad or wish they could still be married, what happens? (What does she do? What do you do?)

D.   (Not included in the child interview.)

E.   If your mom had to choose two things which she wished you didn't feel about the divorce or your dad, what would they be?

When you're feeling or saying something about the divorce which Mom doesn't like, what happens?

Mother-Child Relationship

Some things stay the same for mothers and children after the divorce, and some things become really different, what things are the most different between you and your mom?

Now I'd like to ask you about a few more ways that things might have changed.

Before the divorce, what happened if you did something wrong? (I.e., who dealt with you and in what way?) What happens now? (I.e., what does Mom do?)

What feelings of hers has Mom talked to you about? How is that different than the way things were before the divorce?

What decisions in your family do you help Mom make? How's that different than the way things were before the divorce?

What are your responsibilities in the family, what things do you have to do around the house? Do you have more or less responsibilities now than you did before the divorce?

What happens between you and your mom like at dinner time or when you get home from school? What are things like between you?

How is this different than before the divorce?

In general, do you do more or less with Mom than before the divorce? (Probe for what sorts of things he does more or, less of.)

What things do you do now in your family which Mom used to do?

(For the older child:) What do you do now for your brother/sister which Mom used to do?

(If mother has *not remarried* continue here, otherwise skip to next section.)

Are there people whom mom has spent a lot of time with since the divorce whom she didn't know or see much before the divorce? How much time?

What do you think of them? (Ask for each person.)

How much time do you get to see them?

What do you think of her spending so much time with them?

Do you like having them around? (If you had to vote. . . .)

(If she/he has not mentioned men:) Does your mom go out with men or have a boyfriend now? (Ask again the last five questions about these men.)

Do you and your mom ever talk about him/them? What do you say?

What things do(es) your mom's boyfriend(s) do now that your Dad used to do?

(If mother *has remarried* include this section:)

How did you meet your mom's new husband?

When was that?

What did you feel about him when you first met him?

How did you get to know him?

Did you and your mom ever talk about him? What did you say?

What did you think when Mom first told you she was going to get married again?

What worried you the most about her getting married again?

What do you think of it now?

What things does your stepfather do now that your Dad used to do?

When did he start doing these things?

What are the best things about Mom being married again?

What are the hardest things about Mom being married again?

Are there people whom Mom spent a lot of time with after the divorce whom she didn't know or see much before the divorce, besides her new husband? How much time?

What do you/did you think of them?

What do you/did you think of her spending so much time with them?

Sibling Relationship and Siblings' Reactions

A. We've talked about how moms and how kids your age might react to a divorce. Now I'd like to find out about the reactions of your sister/brother.

You mentioned that your brother/sister felt _____ about the divorce, how else has he/she reacted? (Probe for different time periods—when he first found out there was going to be a divorce, when father first moved out, at the time of the actual divorce, now.)

or

How did x react when he first found out there was going to be a divorce?

How do you think he felt when Dad moved out?

How did he react to the actual divorce when it happened?

How does he feel about the divorce now? How does he show this?

B. How does it make you feel when x _____? (E.g., is sad, gets into a fight with Mom.)

What do you think x feels when you're _____? (Fill in major reactions one at a time.)

How often did you and your brother/sister talk about your feelings about the divorce? What did you talk about?

What are ways a brother and sister (or brothers, sisters) can help each other deal with a divorce?

C. We discussed before how some things stay the same in a family after a divorce and some things become really different. What things are different between you and your brother/sister now?

Again, if I was trying to give advice to someone whose parents were going to get divorced, should I tell him things between a brother and sister (or brothers, sisters) are going to get worse or better after a divorce? Can you tell me more about this?

Would it be harder or easier if you were the only child in the family? Why?

D. You've said that x has been feeling_____. What does Mom do about this?

E. What's the biggest thing that's changed between Mom and x (i.e., in their relationship) since the divorce?

Relationship to Father

A. Tell me about your dad. What's he like?

What are things like between you and your dad since the divorce?

In what ways does he act differently toward you now than before he left home?

B. How often do you see Dad? Where?

What do you do when you visit him?

How often do you talk to him otherwise?

What is it like when you're together?

If you had the choice, would you see him more or less?

How does Mom react when you get together with Dad?

Does she ask about your meetings with Dad? What does she say?

Does she ever get upset or angry before or after your visits with Dad? What about?

C. Tell me about some times when you felt Mom or Dad was pulling you to take their side.

Does Mom or Dad ever ask you questions about what the other is doing or feeling?

Do they ever ask you to give messages from one to the other?

D. What kinds of things does Dad still do for the family?

What's the hardest thing about your dad not living here?

What's easier now that your dad is no longer living with you?

What things do you do now for your mom or your family that your dad used to do?

Does Dad punish you when you do something wrong?

What things does he help you with? Is this different than before the divorce?

E.   Has Dad gotten remarried?

(If father has *not remarried* continue here, otherwise skip to next section:)

Are there people whom dad has spent a lot of time with since the divorce whom he didn't know or see much before the divorce? How much time?

What do you think of them? (Ask for each person.)

How much time do you get to see them?

What do you think of him spending so much time with them?

(If she/he has not mentioned women:) Does your dad go out with women or have a girlfriend now? (Ask again the last four questions about these women.)

Do you and your dad ever talk about her/them? What do you say?

(If father *has remarried* include this section:)

How did you meet your dad's new wife?

When was that?

What did you feel about her when you first met her?

How did you get to know her?

Did you and your dad ever talk about her? What did you say?

What did you think when your dad first told you he was going to get married again?

What worried you the most about him getting married again?

What do you think of it now?

What things does your stepmother do that are like what a mom does?

Are there people besides his new wife whom dad spent a lot of time with after the divorce whom he didn't know or see much before the divorce? How much time?

What do you/did you think of them?

What did you/do you think of him spending so much time with them?

F.   What were things like between Dad and Mom when you were little?

Do you remember them getting angry at each other a lot? How did they show that?

How were things getting between them just before the divorce?

(If there is any indication of trouble noted, but not described, in the marriage:) What things made you think they were having trouble with each other? (I.e., in what ways did they show that they weren't getting along so well?)

What do you think are the real reasons why they got divorced?

How do they act towards each other now?

Notes

Chapter 2

1. These numbers do not correspond to who is listed as the plaintiff in the court records. Women are listed plaintiff in almost all cases on file in Washtenaw County regardless of who actually insisted on the divorce. It was related that lawyers generally encourage this because it supposedly helps a woman postdivorce in such matters as obtaining a good credit rating.

2. All names are fictitious.

3. Only one such case came to light in all the court files examined. The discrepancy between these findings and those of Westman may be due to differences in time (ten years) or court systems. In general, far fewer families in Washtenaw County (52 percent in Westman's sample) became involved in any legal contest after the divorce was finalized.

4. In comparison to the sample studied by Wallerstein and Kelly (1980), the number of women participating in this research who were living with a man is low. At the time of their first follow-up interview, one and one-half years after the separation (i.e., approximately the same number of months since the divorce as the current interviews), Wallerstein and Kelly found that 17 percent of the women had remarried (in contrast to 10 percent in the present study) and about the same percentage shared their home with a live-in male friend or another single-parent family (in contrast to 12 percent in the present study).

5. It is significant that fathers remarry more quickly than mothers. Twelve fathers (i.e., 30 percent) as compared with four mothers (i.e., 10 percent) had remarried by the time of the interview. One more had definite marriage plans. Similarly, six men had live-in girlfriends (one of whom was included in the remarried group as he is now divorced again and involved with someone new). Children are involved in these weddings and the plans for them to varying degrees. It is common for the fathers to inform the children of the marriage, often through the mother, only after it has taken place. In contrast, all the children affected were minutely involved in their mother's wedding.

   Wallerstein and Kelly (1980) also found that the divorced fathers in their study remarried more quickly than the mothers although the differences between the sexes was far smaller than for the current sample. At the time of the first follow-up interview, 20 percent of the men as compared with 17 percent of the women had remarried.

6. It appears from the above tabulations that this sample differs from that of Carolyn Stoloff (1979) who drew her subjects from the same county population. She reported that a high percentage of her sample had worked prior to the divorce and concluded that she was studying a rather untraditional sample or that working women were more likely to divorce.

Although it is possible that Dr. Stoloff's sample was skewed in the direction of working women because of the nature of her study (i.e., a questionnaire administered through the mail), it seems more likely that a probe into the role that work had played in these women's lives and the sequence of events regarding the considering of divorce and the return to work would show that her sample was similar to the present one.

7. The frequency of visitation cannot be determined from the court files. Actual practice frequently differs from what is stated in the settlement. Furthermore, in most cases, it is simply written that the father has "reasonable" visitation rights. "Reasonable" has numerous interpretations.

8. Wallerstein and Kelly do not report the frequency of visits at the time of their follow-up interview (i.e., the time period comparable to the one studied in the present research). However, they noted that at the time of the initial interview, 40 percent of the children were seeing their father at least once a week. A little more than 25 percent of the children had contact with their father two or three times a month. The duration of each visit ranged from a few hours to an overnight stay. The remaining children were visited less than once a month on an unpredictable basis. In the five years following the separation, Wallerstein and Kelly found that, in general, a gradual decrease in the visiting frequency had occurred but no sharp declines were evident.

In contrast, Hetherington (1977) related that after a brief effort to maintain a great deal of contact shortly following the separation, a rapid decline in visits was evident for the children in her sample. She does not report the exact frequency of visitation for any time period. It seems likely that Hetherington's findings relate to the young age of the children studied, that is, that fathers demonstrate greater interest in maintaining close contact with older children.

Chapter 3

1. The women were interviewed anytime from approximately one-half a year to one and one-half years following their divorce. The amount of time which had elapsed since the divorce was certainly a factor affecting a woman's view in that on average, mothers who had reorganized their lives were divorced longer (mean number of months since the divorce: 14.5) than mothers in either of the other two groups (10.6 months and 11.2 months respectively). However, time is not the only important variable here. The many factors examined in the previous chapter also impact on the speed with which a mother achieves stability postdivorce.

Chapter 4

1. Although the children commonly responded in the third person due to the phrasing of the questions (as explained in chapter 2), it was assumed in presenting the material for this chapter that the children's descriptions, except in a few obvious instances, applied to their own mothers. In fact, as will be evident in some quotes, many children started talking in the third person and gradually switched to statements like "my mother said." They also interjected comments about their "own family" in explanations largely referring to what mothers in general might feel.

Appendix A

1. This decision resulted in the elimination of only two potential subjects, both of whom had annual incomes a few thousand dollars below the established cutoff.

2. The unexpected difficulty encountered in reaching potential subjects was due to the high number of instances in which calling the person resulted in learning that the phone had been disconnected or that the telephone number found in the county court records was no longer correct. Trouble learning a person's new telephone number was not due to a change in listing from the mother's married to her maiden name as the latter name was known from the state records. Two women were found to have a new number listed under their maiden name. Similarly, if a woman had moved within the county boundaries or only slightly outside of them a forwarding number was provided by the operator. The lack of a forwarding number indicated that the family had moved a distance out of town, had chosen to have an unlisted number (this was also stated by the operator and happened in just one case) or that the mother had moved *and* remarried.

3. Initially, even more women said that they would take part but two (20 percent of the total refusals, N = 10) called back to cancel because their children became upset when the interview was mentioned and one (10 percent of refusals) found out that she was moving out of state two weeks earlier than she had predicted and thus before the interview could take place. Four others (40 percent of total refusals) responded by saying that they would gladly participate themselves but did not want the children to take part, feeling it would be upsetting for them.

Bibliography

Anthony, E. J. Children at Risk from Divorce: A Review. In *The Child in His Family: Children at Psychiatric Risk*, III. Edited by E. J. Anthony and Koupernik, C. New York: John Wiley & Sons, 1974.

Bernstein, M. R. & Robey, J. S. "Detection and Management of the Pediatric Difficulties Created by Divorce." *Pediatrics* 30 (1962):950–56.

Bohannan, P. The Six Stations of Divorce. In P. Bohannan (Ed.), *Divorce and After*. New York: Doubleday, 1968.

Brandwein, R., Brown, C., and Fox, E. "Women and Children Last: the Social Situation of Divorced Mothers and their Families." *Journal of Marriage and the Family* 36 (1974):498–514.

Burchinal, L. G. "Characteristics of Adolescents from Unbroken, Broken and Reconstructed Families." *Journal of Marriage and the Family* 26 (1964):44–51.

Burn, G. "The Child of Divorce in Denmark." *Bulletin of the Menninger Clinic* 28 (1964):2–10.

Despert, L. *Children of Divorce*. New York: Doubleday, 1953.

Dorpat, T. L., Jackson, J. K., and Ripley, H. J. "Broken Homes and Attempted and Completed Suicides." *Archives of General Psychiatry* 12 (1965):213–16.

Epstein, J. *Divorced in America*. New York: E.P. Dutton, 1974.

Fulton, J. A. "Parental Reports of Children's Postdivorce Adjustment." *Journal of Social Issues* 35 (1979):126–39.

Gardner, G. E. "Separation of the Parents and the Emotional Life of the Child." *Mental Hygiene* 40 (1956):53–64.

Gardner, R. A. *Psychotherapy with Children of Divorce*. New York: Jason Aronson, 1976.

Glasser, P., & Navarre, E. "Structural Problems of the One-Parent Family." *Journal of Social Issues* 21 (1965):89–109.

Goode, W. J. Family Disorganization. In *Contemporary Social Problems*. Edited by R. K. Merton and R. A. Nisbett. New York: Harcourt & Brace, 1961.

_____. *Women in Divorce*. New York: The Free Press, 1956.

Hetherington, E. M. "Effects of Father Absence on Personality Development in Adolescent Daughters." *Developmental Psychology* 7 (1972):313–26.

Hetherington, E. M., Cox, M., and Cox, R. "Beyond Father Absence: Conceptualizations of Effects of Divorce." In *Contemporary Readings in Child Psychology*. Edited by E. M. Hetherington and R.D. Parke. New York: McGraw-Hill, 1977.

_____. "The Aftermath of Divorce." In *Mother-Child, Father-Child Relations*. Edited by J. H. Stevens, Jr. and M. Mathews. Washington, D.C.: N.A.E.Y.C., 1978.

_____. "Family Interaction and the Social, Emotional, and Cognitive Development of Children Following Divorce." Presented at the Symposium on the Family: Setting Priorities, Washington, D.C., 1978.

_____. "Play and Social Interaction in Children Following Divorce." Presented at the National Institute of Mental Health's Conference on Divorce, Washington, D.C., 1978.

Jacobson, D. S. "The Impact of Marital Separation/Divorce on Children: I Parent-Child Separation and Child Adjustment." *Journal of Divorce* 1 (1978):341-60.

_____. "The Impact of Marital Separation/Divorce on Children: II Interparent Hostility and Child Adjustment." *Journal of Divorce* 2 (1978):3-19.

Kalter, N. "Children of Divorce in an Outpatient Psychiatric Population." *American Journal of Orthopsychiatry* 47 (1977):40-51.

Kelly, J. B. "Children and Parents in the Midst of Divorce: Some Factors Contributing to Differentiated Response." By invitation, National Institute of Mental Health, 1977.

Kelly, J. B. and Wallerstein, J. S. "The Effects of Parental Divorce: Experiences of the Child in Early Latency." *American Journal of Orthopsychiatry* 46 (1976):20-32.

Landis, J. "The Trauma of Children When Parents Divorce." *Journal of Marriage and Family Living* 22 (1960):7-13.

_____. "A Comparison of Children from Divorced and Nondivorced Unhappy Marriages." *The Family Life Coordinator* 11 (1962):61-65.

_____. "Social Correlates of Divorce and Nondivorce among the Unhappy Married." *Journal of Marriage and Family Living* 25 (1963):1978-80.

McDermott, J. "Parental Divorce in Early Childhood." *American Journal of Psychiatry* 124 (1968):1424-32.

_____. "Divorce and its Psychiatric Sequel in Children." *Archives of General Psychiatry* 23 (1970):421-27.

Messer, A. A. "Dissolution of Longstanding Marriages." *Mental Hygiene* 53 (1969):127-30.

Miller, A. A. Reactions of friends to divorce. In *Divorce and after*. Edited by P. Bohannan. New York: Doubleday, 1968.

Morrison, J. E. "Parental Divorce as a Factor in Childhood Psychiatric Illness." *Comprehensive Psychiatry* 15 (1974) 95-102.

Nye, I. "Child Adjustment in Broken and Unhappy, Unbroken Homes." *Journal of Marriage and Family Living* 19 (1957):356-61.

Otterstrom, E. "Social Outlook for Children of Divorcees." *Acta Genetica* 3 (1952):72-96.

Roberts, A. R. and Roberts, B. J. Divorce and the Child: A Pyrrhic Victory. In *Childhood Deprivation*. Edited by A.R. Roberts. Springfield: C.C. Thomas, 1974.

Robinson, et al. "Children of Separated Parents." *Medical Journal of Australia* 2 (1973):899-902.

Scanzoni, J. "A Social System Analysis of Dissolved and Existing Marriages." *Journal of Marriage and the Family* 30 (1968):452-62.

Stoloff, C. "The Impact of Changing Social, Sexual and Occupational Contexts on Recently Divorced Women." Ph.D. dissertation, University of Michigan, 1979.

Sugar, M. "Children of Divorce." *Pediatrics* 46 (1970):588-95.

_____. "Divorce and Children." *Southern Medical Journal* 3 (1970):1458-61.

Tooley, K. "The Man of the House and His Mother: Antisocial Behavior and Social Alienation Postdivorce." *American Journal of Orthopsychiatry* 46 (1976):33-42.

Toomin, M. K. The Child of Divorce. In *Therapeutic Needs of the Family: Problems, Descriptions, and Therapeutic Approaches*. Springfield: Charles C. Thomas, 1974.

U.S. Bureau of the Census. *Statistical abstracts of the United States: 1982-83*. Washington, D.C.: U.S. Department of Commerce, 1983.

Waddle, C. J. "Two Generations of Broken Homes in the Genesis of Conduct and Behavior Disorders in Childhood." *British Medical Journal* 2 (1961):349.

Wallerstein, J. S. "Children and Parents 18 Months after Parental Separation: Factors Related to Differential Outcome." Unpublished. 1977.

_____. "The Effects of Parental Divorce: Experiences of the Preschool Child." *Journal of the American Academy of Child Psychiatry* 14 (1975):600–616.

_____. "The Effects of Parental Divorce: Experiences of the Child in Later Latency." *American Journal of Orthopsychiatry* 46 (1976):256–69.

_____. *Surviving the Breakup: How Children and Parents Cope with Divorce.* New York: Basic Books, 1980.

Wallerstein, J. S. and Kelly, J. B. The Effects of Parental Divorce: The Adolescent Experience. In *The Child in His Family: Children at Psychiatric Risk,* III. Edited by E. J. Anthony and C. Koupernik. New York: John Wiley & Sons, 1974.

Weiss, R. S. *Marital Separation.* New York: Basic Books, 1975.

_____. *Going It Alone: The Family Life and Social Situation of the Single Parent.* New York: Basic Books, 1979.

Westman, J. C., Cline, D. W., Swift, W. J., & Kramer, D. A. "The Role of Child Psychiatry in Divorce." *Archives of General Psychiatry* 23 (1970):416–20.

Westman, J. C. "Effects of Divorce on a Child's Personality Development." *Medical Aspects of Human Sexuality* 6 (1972):38–55.

Wylie, H. L. and Delgado, R. A. "A Pattern of Mother-Son Relationship Involving the Absence of the Father." *American Journal of Orthopsychiatry* 29 (1959):644–49.

Index